Second Edition, first published in the United States of America in 2020 by
Universe Publishing, a division of Rizzoli International Publications, Inc.
300 Park Avenue South, New York, NY 10010
www.rizzoliusa.com
First edition published in 2014 and revised and updated in 2017

Created by olo.éditions /www.oloeditions.com /36, rue Laffitte, 75009 Paris, France

Original concept / Marçais&Marchand
Editorial direction / Nicolas Marçais
Art direction / Philippe Marchand
Author / Bernard Lions
Layout / Marion Alfano, ZS studio
Editor / Nicolas Camus, ZS studio

English translation / Roland Glasser
Shirt design / S2 Synergy Global
Proofreaders / Jonah Fontela, Aurélie Gaillot, Jeannie Ng

Library of Congress Control Number: 2019956517
ISBN-13: 978-0-7893-3775-7
2020 2021 2022 2023/10 9 8 7 6 5 4 3 2 1
Printed in Bosnia and Herzegovina

Acknowledgements
olo.éditions would like to thank all of the trademark holders (clubs, national associations, manufacturers, sponsors etc.) for the visuals reproduced in this work.
Thank you as well to Thierry Freiberg, David Ausseil, and Charles-Henry Contamine for their help. The author would like to thank Patrick Battiston, Cyprien Cini (France, RTL), Bruno Constant (England), Garance Ferreaux (France, M6), Eric Frosio (Brazil), Stéphane Guy (France, Canal +), Franck Le Dorze (France, L'Equipe), Bixente Lizarazu, Roque Gaston Maspoli, Jean-Pierre Papin, Sergueï Polkhovski (Ukraine), Johnny Rep, Jean-Michel Rouet (France, L'Equipe), Alexis Menuge (Germany), Manuel Queiros (Portugal), Florent Torchut (Argentina), and Marie Yuuki (Japan).

Preamble
In order to ensure a uniform appearance, all of the shirts have been redrawn in the most realistic manner possible. Where a particular shirt was worn during a season spanning two calendar years, the dates used in captions refer to the year in which the season finished (i.e. "2020" instead of "2019-20"). The honours listed are correct as of the end of the 2018-19 season.
The international and continental honours only include the results achieved in the following competitions: FIFA World Cup, FIFA Confederations Cup, Copa América, Pan American Championship, Olympic Games, UEFA European Football Championship, Gold Cup, African Cup of Nations, AFC Asian Cup, FIFA Women's World Cup, UEFA Champions League (including the former European Cup), UEFA Europa League (including the former UEFA Cup and Inter-Cities Fairs Cup), UEFA Cup Winners' Cup, UEFA Super Cup, Intercontinental Cup, FIFA Club World Cup, Copa Libertadores, Supercopa Libertadores, Recopa Sudamericana, Copa Sudamericana and Copa CONMEBOL.
In the first section of the book, the order in which national teams appear is based first and foremost on their performances at the World Cup, and then at other international tournaments. The order in which clubs appear is based first and foremost on their performances in non-domestic tournaments.
In the second section of the book, nations are listed according to the ranking defined by the International Federation of Football History & Statistics (IFFHS).
In the event of readers discovering any errors, they should not hesitate to write to: contact@oloeditions.com so that they can be corrected in future editions.

1000 football shirts

THE COLOURS OF THE BEAUTIFUL GAME

Bernard Lions

foreword by
Carlo Ancelotti

UNIVERSE

I was Tagnin. Dreaming of Di Stéfano.

was not as chubby as I am now. Back then my heart was clearly visible under a thin layer of skin. More than feel it, you could see it pounding. We're talking about the beating heart of a six-year-old child who had just been given his first football shirt. Pure emotion. Even then I was called Carletto, but that day I was not Ancelotti. I was Tagnin; defensive midfielder who, at Prater Stadium in Vienna only a few months before, had taken the legendary, luminary Alfredo Di Stéfano out of the European cup final. The shirt was that of Inter, my first love, overwhelming passion and memorable better half (or rather my better third, because my size has over time become cumbersome, invading other people's space...) and the shirt that, for work, I had to leave behind.

Made from a heavy fabric, the shirt was so hot that it overwhelmed me in the winter and in the summer risked hospitalising me for suffocation, yet it was my formula for happiness. A suit of armour against everyone and everything. Soaked to capacity during lightning storms and abominable when the sun was out. Its fibres overlapped, running, rebelling, and tangling around me. Maybe I scratched, but I kept smiling, because you cannot be allergic to beauty.

The lines were very thick, black as the fear that overwhelmed opponents, and as blue as the sky, and the secret was right there: to compose the best stories, you do not need an infinite number of pages; a few lines are sufficient. Those lines. Some sweet emotions can also be written vertically. They had not yet added the numbers, nor the names to be stuck on the back, and it was all so perfect: a diamond, to be such, must remain raw. Any impurities will ruin its elegance.

That for me was the shirt and will remain so forever. To be used during the games of the imagination, on a field of dirt in which I saw the finely cut grass of the San Siro. Surrounded by the purest thoughts. As a player first and then as a manager, the colours would change, the boundaries also, the prospects as well, but the first love is never forgotten. Not a collector's item, simply a piece of my heart. I was Tagnin. Dreaming of Di Stéfano.

Carlo ANCELOTTI
Manager of Napoli, 2018–
(Former player for Parma, Roma, and AC Milan, and
former manager of Reggiana, Parma, Juventus, AC Milan,
Chelsea F.C., Paris Saint-Germain, Real Madrid FC, and Bayern Munich)

Contents

Notts County FC, the oldest football club in the world still playing at a professional level. The club was founded in 1862. (Group photograph taken in 1905.)

Brazil
Italy
Germany
Argentina
Uruguay
France
Spain
England
Mexico
Russia
Cameroon
Japan
Netherlands
United States

215
Legendary Shirts

Boca Juniors
FC Barcelona
Real Madrid
Ajax
Liverpool
Juventus
Internazionale
Bayern Munich
Santos
FC Porto
Manchester United
Chelsea
Borussia Dortmund
Benfica
Paris Saint-Germain

Roger Milla couldn't help himself. When the final whistle signaled the end of Cameroon's historic win over Argentina in Italia 90's opening game, the thirty-eight-year-old Indomitable Lion chased after Maradona and asked for his jersey. With the shock of defeat still fresh, the Argentine icon offered up his stripes gladly, with a smile, draping Milla's green shirt across his own shoulders.

Some shirts remain forever connected to the great ones who wore them— Alfredo Di Stéfano in the pure white of Madrid, Maradona in the light blue of Napoli, Cruyff in his bright orange, Zidane all in royal, blazing blue. Even for the greatest players, a football jersey stirs emotions. On pitches across the world, players swap them with opponents. Sometimes after a glorious victory, sometimes in the doldrums of defeat, and sometimes even at halftime with the game still in the balance! These shirts often end up in frames, behind glass, and hanging in homes, cherished symbols of past battles.

The sight of players swapping shirts at the end of a match is now commonplace, but that was not the case until May 31, 1931. The French, delighted to have beaten the English for the first time in ten years, asked if they could keep their opponents' jerseys as a souvenir of the match. This sporting behaviour later gained worldwide acceptance when Pelé and Bobby Moore swapped shirts at the final whistle of Brazil's hard-fought 1–0 win over England on June 7, 1970, at the World Cup in Mexico. While swapping shirts at the end of a game is now customary, taking off a shirt during a game to celebrate a goal or for almost any other reason is considered unsportsmanlike behaviour and prohibited by FIFA.

Of course, there are some memorable exceptions. When Chelsea played against Reading on October 14, 2006, both goalkeeper Cech and substitute goalkeeper Cudicini left the field with injuries. Captain and central defender John Terry put on a goalkeeper's jersey and finished the game between the uprights. On April 13, 1996, Sir Alex Ferguson, down 3–0 against Southampton, made his Manchester United players switch shirts at halftime, blaming the kit's grey colour for the team's poor performance. It almost worked. They got one goal back but still ended up losing the game.

Shirts do so much more than tell the history of football. They speak of legend. They stand for entire eras, stoking memories and dreams of impossible matches and unforgettable teams.

White is no longer cursed

THE *SELEÇÃO* BEGAN THEIR COPA AMÉRICA 2019 IN WHITE, A COLOUR THAT HAD BEEN CURSED FOR NEARLY SEVENTY YEARS. IT DID NOT STOP THEM FROM WINNING, HOWEVER.

When the Brazilian Football Federation (CBF) announced that the Seleção would celebrate the centenary of their first victory in the Copa América by playing the opening match against Bolivia in white (3–0), the Brazilians' blood suddenly ran cold. Although white had been the original colour of Brazil's shirt, it had been cursed since July 16, 1950, when Uruguay deprived them of a final victory in "their" FIFA World Cup (1–2). This traumatic defeat went down in history as the *Maracanaçao* (the Agony at Maracanã). Neymar's right-ankle injury during the final preparation match against Qatar (2–0 on June 6, 2019) seemed to confirm this jinx.

Despite playing without their number 10, Brazil managed finally to drive the curse away by beating Peru in the final (3–1 on July 7, 2019). That evening, the Seleção wore retro *auriverde* (gold and green) uniforms, with a green polo collar, honouring the victory of 1989, which was also won at home. Green symbolises the Amazonian forests, and yellow, the gold deposits of a country that has won four of its five World Cups with the *Canarinha* (Little Canary) kit, having won its first in 1958, in the colour blue, in Sweden.

10
GLOBAL HONOURS
5 FIFA World Cups
4 FIFA Confederations Cups
1 Olympic Games

9
CONTINENTAL HONOURS
9 Copas América

2002
World Cup–
winning jersey

1950
World Cup–
runners-up jersey

1958
World Cup–
winning jersey

1962
World Cup–
winning jersey

1994
World Cup–
winning jersey

Pelé, number 10 by chance

Players have not always performed with a number on their back, let alone a name. Introduced during the 1930s in England, systematic numbering was formalised by FIFA at the 1954 World Cup. And it was not until the 1958 tournament in Sweden that the number 10 came to symbolise the team's most creative player, due to a seventeen-year-old debutant named Pelé and a bureaucratic error by the Brazilian FA. Before the start of the competition, Brazil's football powers sent in the list of selected players, as required, but they forgot to allocate specific jersey numbers to the players. A FIFA delegate from Uruguay took charge, rather obliviously handing the number 3 shirt to the first-choice goalkeeper, Gilmar, and the 10 to the hitherto unknown Pelé. Injured in the run-up to the global gathering, Pelé made his first appearance during the third match against USSR and went on to score six goals in four matches. He scored three times in the 5–2 win over France during the semifinal and twice over Sweden in the final, Brazil winning again 5–2. And so the legend of the number 10 was born. By chance.

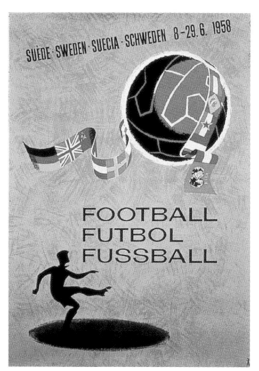

MEXICO CITY (MEXICO), AZTECA STADIUM
JUNE 21, 1970
Pelé celebrates in Jairzinho's arms after guiding Brazil into a lead in the World Cup final against Italy.

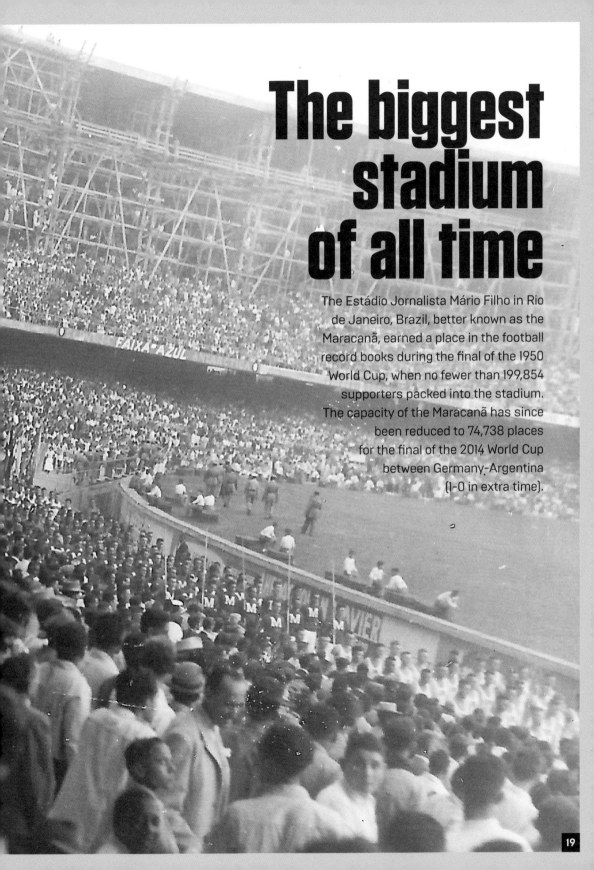

The biggest stadium of all time

The Estádio Jornalista Mário Filho in Rio de Janeiro, Brazil, better known as the Maracanã, earned a place in the football record books during the final of the 1950 World Cup, when no fewer than 199,854 supporters packed into the stadium. The capacity of the Maracanã has since been reduced to 74,738 places for the final of the 2014 World Cup between Germany-Argentina (1-0 in extra time).

Germany

Reunited and multicultural

REUNITED AFTER THE FALL OF THE BERLIN WALL IN 1989, THE NATIONALMANNSCHAFT TOOK ADVANTAGE OF A NEW NATIONALITY LAW TO BECOME MORE MULTICULTURAL.

Although the German flag is black, red, and yellow, the national team play in nineteenth century Prussian colours: white with black shorts. A national symbol since the twelfth century, the eagle is a reference to the Holy Roman Empire. Separation came after World War II, and from 1949 to 1990 two different jerseys were worn by two different German teams: FRG (west) and GDR (east). In 1974, the World Cup came to West Germany, and the two teams played each other in Hamburg. East Germany won 1–0. Although reunification (October 3, 1990) allowed Matthias Sammer, a future European Footballer of the Year winner (in 1996), to become the first East German to play for the Nationalmannschaft, the new Germany failed to perform at the very highest level. Euro 1996 and the 2014 World Cup still remain the only tournaments won since reunification. All three other German World Cups were won by those west of the great divide. Germany's 3–0 defeat by Croatia at the 1998 World Cup forced a rethink of the national setup. The nationality law of January 1, 2000, which granted citizenship to all people born in the country, has allowed second-generation players—such as Boateng, Khedira, and Özil—to emerge.

6

GLOBAL HONOURS
4 FIFA World Cups
1 Olympic Games (GDR)
1 Olympic Games (RDA)

3

CONTINENTAL HONOURS
3 UEFA European Football Championships

2014
World Cup–
winning jersey

1954
FRG
World Cup–
winning jersey

1974
FRG
World Cup–
winning jersey

1974
GDR
jersey worn
during World Cup

1990
FRG
FIFA World Cup–
winning jersey

Germany

The number 13, lucky for some

BERLIN (GERMANY), OLYMPIASTADION
OCTOBER 16, 2012
Wearing 13 on his back, Thomas Müller was named Best Young Player at the 2010 World Cup in South Africa.

HAMBURG (GERMANY), VOLKSPARKSTADION
JUNE 22, 1974
West German skipper Franz Beckenbauer shakes hands with his East German counterpart Bernd Bransch before the only official match ever played between the two nations.

All players believe their little superstitions and habits give them an extra edge on the pitch. Few, for example, like to wear the number 13 shirt. In Christianity, Judas is synonymous with the number 13. The betrayer of Jesus was the thirteenth guest at the table of the Last Supper.

And so it is strange that in Germany, with its two-thirds Christian population, wearers of the number 13 jersey have enjoyed great luck. In 1954, Max Morlock, wearing number 13, scored six goals in five matches at the World Cup in Switzerland. This included the goal that launched the comeback against Hungary in the fourth of July final. The Germans were down 2–0 and went on to win 3–2.

At the 1970 World Cup, Gerd Müller, also wearing 13, scored ten goals in six matches. Four years later "Bomber 13" scored the winning goal in the final and gave the hosts a 2–1 victory over the Netherlands on July 7, 1974. The goal, his fourteenth and last in the World Cup, saw him overtake Frenchman Just Fontaine's record of 13 (all scored at the 1958 finals). The record stood until 2006, when the Brazilian Ronaldo bagged fifteen. In 2002, Michael Ballack, with 13 on his back, scored the only goal against the United States in the quarterfinals and against South Korea in the semifinals. Ballack was suspended for the final, and Germany lost 2–0 against Brazil on June 30.

At the 2010 World Cup, the number 13 jersey was worn by twenty-year-old Thomas Müller, who finished the tournament as joint top-scorer with five goals, and was also named its Best Young Player.

"Football is a simple game; 22 men chase a ball for 90 minutes and, at the end, the Germans win."

Gary Lineker

(England captain and 1986 World Cup Golden Boot winner, after losing the 1990 World Cup semifinal to Germany on penalties)

Gerd Müller is lifted in triumph after his winning goal against the Dutch in the World Cup final.

Italy

Green, white, and red = blue

FOUR-TIME WORLD CUP WINNERS ITALY ARE ONE OF THE FEW TEAMS NOT TO PLAY IN THE COLOURS OF THEIR NATIONAL FLAG.

Known by Italian fans as *La Nazionale*, the team was renamed *La Squadra Azzurra* (the Blue Team) by French journalists during the World Cup in 1938, held in France. Originally, Italy played in white, one of the three colours of their national flag (along with green and red). Their first official international, on May 15, 1910, was played in white against France at the Milan Arena. Italy won 6–2. But just eight months later against Hungary on January 6, 1911, they put on a different coloured shirt, a blue shirt. The colour, a seemingly strange pick, was chosen in honour of the royal family of the House of Savoy, whose official colour is blue. And Italy hasn't looked back, becoming known as the *Azzurri*. All other Italian national teams followed suit, choosing blue as their colour. The white of old is used as a second strip, allowing Italians to remember their sporting origins.

5
GLOBAL HONOURS
4 FIFA World Cups
1 Olympic Games

1
CONTINENTAL HONOUR
1 UEFA European Football Championship

2006
World Cup–
winning jersey

1910
First jersey

1934-38
Two-time World Cup–
winning jersey

1968
European
Championship–
winning jersey

1982
World Cup–
winning jersey

**BERLIN (GERMANY),
OLYMPIASTADION**
JULY 9, 2006
Italy captain Fabio
Cannavaro hoists his
nation's fourth World Cup
after victory over France.

The Balotelli conundrum

Known for his hijinks during his time at Manchester City (2010 to January 2013), Mario Balotelli has a similar history with the Italian national team. During a friendly against Uruguay on November 15, 2011, at Rome's Stadio Olimpico, the Azzurri striker came on at halftime wearing the wrong jersey. He had put on an older shirt, something that posed a problem since the match had been organised to promote the new Puma-designed jersey ahead of Euro 2012. The referee did not take long to notice. At the first stoppage in play following an aerial clash with La Celeste captain Diego Perez, the referee asked Balotelli to change into the same shirt as his teammates.

"I'm Italian, I feel Italian, I'll always play for the Italian national team."

Mario Balotelli

WARSAW (POLAND), NATIONAL STADIUM
JUNE 28, 2012
"Super Mario" strikes his trademark pose after scoring a second against Germany in the Euro 2012 semifinal.

Argentinian alphabet

UP UNTIL THE 1986 WORLD CUP, THE ARGENTINIAN FA WERE IN THE HABIT OF ASSIGNING NUMBERS BASED ON PLAYERS' SURNAMES. THE 10 WORN BY THE LEGENDARY MARADONA WAS AN EXCEPTION.

When dressing-room superstitions and wheeling and dealing are taken into account, allocating player numbers can be a headache for football authorities. The Argentinian Football Association (AFA) thought it had found a solution to the problem when, during the World Cups of 1974, 1978, and 1982, they distributed numbers in alphabetical order, using players' family names as a guide. Number 1, therefore, went to attacking midfielders Norberto Alonso (aka Beto) in 1978 and Ossie Ardiles in 1982, and then to attacker Sergio Almirón in 1986. Goalkeeper Ubaldo Fillol received the 12, followed by the 5 and the 7. But there were some exceptions to this very Argentinian rule in 1982. Mario Kempes, number 13 in 1974, should have kept the 10 he wore when his country became world champions in 1978, which would have given Maradona the 12. But the national icon managed to keep hold of the 10, and Kempes wore 11 in the end. The system all but fell apart at the 1986 World Cup in Mexico. Captain Daniel Passarella demanded the number 6 jersey that served him so well at club level, while Jorge Valdano wanted the 11. The AFA was eventually forced to give in to the players. It all worked out for the best, however, as the Albiceleste won the prestigious trophy for a second time that year.

5

GLOBAL HONOURS
2 FIFA World Cups
1 FIFA Confederations Cup
2 Olympic Games

14

CONTINENTAL HONOURS
14 Copas América

1986
World Cup–
winning jersey

1930
World Cup–
runners-up jersey

1978
World Cup–
winning jersey

1994
Jersey worn by Maradona
when he scored his last
goal for the national team

2006
First jersey worn
by Messi during the
World Cup

Argentina

From Maradona to Messi

Suddenly, the Argentinian supporters in Hamburg's World Cup Stadium turned away from their young number 10, Lionel Messi, who was doing his bit to beat a strong Ivory Coast side 2–1 in the opening Group C match of the 2006 finals (June 10). Their eyes were now fixed on another 10, "El Diez." And as the German cameras broadcast the arrival of the great Diego Armando Maradona onto the arena's giant screens, the crowd began long, appreciative chants: "Diego! Diego!"

The match became, in that moment, an afterthought. Until Messi, no player had truly managed to fill Maradona's shoes in the eyes of the Argentinian people, to the extent that on November 14, 2001, more than seven years after awarding him his ninety-first and final cap in a 2–1 win over Nigeria on June 25, 1994, the AFA decided to retire his number 10 jersey.

After reaching an agreement with the 2002 World Cup Local Organising Committee, the AFA drew up a list of twenty-three players, numbered 1 to 24. But FIFA rejected it. Article 26, paragraph 4, of the governing body's regulations requires players to wear the numbers 1 to 23. FIFA President Sepp Blatter suggested giving the 10 to Roberto Bonano, the third-choice goalkeeper, but it was finally allotted to Ariel Ortega, who had already worn the famous number at the 1998 World Cup. Subsequently, Pablo Aimar and Juan Riquelme took a turn, but it was the emergence of Messi, who made his debut in a friendly with Hungary on August 17, 2005, that would finally solve the "problem." Messi is the only player that Maradona, who inherited the number 10 jersey from the mighty Mario Kempes, sees as his rightful successor in the Argentinian national side.

MEXICO CITY (MEXICO), ESTADIO AZTECA
JUNE 22, 1986
Diego Maradona reaches above England goalkeeper Peter Shilton to punch home his famous "Hand of God" goal for Argentina in the quarterfinal of the World Cup.

After dribbling past six opponents and a 60-yard run, Maradona scores the 'Goal of the Century.'

"Maradona on the ball now. Two closing him down. Maradona rolls his foot over the ball ...

and breaks away down the right. He goes past a third, looks for Burruchaga.

Maradona forever! Genius! Genius! Genius! He's still going... Gooooal!

Sorry, I want to cry! Good God! Long live football!"

[Victor Hugo Morales's commentary—Radio Continental, Argentina].

37

Cock-a-doodle-don't

IT MAY JUST BE A CURIOUS COINCIDENCE, BUT FRANCE SAW SOME OF ITS DARKEST DAYS WHEN THE ROOSTER ON ITS SHIRT WAS NOT FACING TOWARDS THE HEART BUT RATHER AWAY FROM IT.

This might seem like an easily missed detail, yet the consequences have been dramatic. Immediately after their defeat in the 2006 World Cup final against Italy (1–1, then 3–5 on penalties), the rooster, the proud symbol of the French team since 1909, took a strange pirouette and switched direction to look outwards (to the player's left). Wearing this new shirt, upon which the rooster turned its back on the heart, *Les Bleus* (the Blues) entered the darkest period in their history. In addition to their elimination from the group stages of UEFA Euro 2008 and the 2010 World Cup, France's image was tarnished by the players' revolt in South Africa, and Samir Nasri's insults directed at a journalist after France's elimination from the quarterfinals of Euro 2012 at the hands of Spain (0–2). It was as if the whole team had lost their heads. Things changed only when the rooster returned to its original position, following qualification for the 2014 World Cup. With their emblems looking them straight in the hearts again, Les Bleus were finalists on home soil in Euro 2016 (0–1 in extra time against Portugal), before winning a second World Cup in 2018.

2010
Jersey worn at World Cup with the rooster not facing toward the heart

5
GLOBAL HONOURS
2 FIFA World Cups
2 FIFA Confederations Cups
1 Olympic Games

2
CONTINENTAL HONOURS
2 UEFA European Football Championships

2018
World Cup–
winning jersey

1904
First jersey

1909-14
White jersey with
blue-and-white
stripes

1958
Jersey worn
at World Cup

1998
FIFA World Cup–
winning jersey

France

The billion-euro men

Lloris (cap.)

Pavard Varane Umtiti Hernández

Tolisso Kanté Pogba

Dembélé Griezmann

Mbappé

In 2018, France won its second World Cup title and became the most expensive team in history. Four Frenchmen dominated the top six places of the top ten in 2019, behind Neymar's €222 million): Kylian Mbappé (second); Antoine Griezmann (tied for third with Brazil's Philippe Coutinho); Ousmane Dembélé (fifth), whose €105 million transfer fee was accompanied by a €54 million bonus; and Paul Pogba (sixth).

The starting eleven for the first match of the 2018 World Cup against Australia (2–1):

A €906.50 M ELEVEN

Hugo Lloris: €12.6 M
(Olympique Lyon to Tottenham Spurs, August 31, 2012).
MV: €25 M

Benjamin Pavard: €35 M
(Stuttgart to Bayern Munich, July 1, 2019)

Raphaël Varane: €10 M
(Lens to Real Madrid, July 1, 2011). MV: €70 M

Samuel Umtiti: €25 M
(Olympique Lyon to FC Barcelona, July 12, 2016). MV: €45 M

Lucas Hernández: €80 M
(Atlético de Madrid to Bayern Munich, July 1, 2019)

Corentin Tolisso: €41.50 M
(Olympique Lyon to Bayern Munich, July 1, 2017)

N'Golo Kanté: €35.80 M
(Leicester to Chelsea, July 16, 2016). MV: €100 M

Paul Pogba: €105 M
(Juventus FC to Manchester United, August 9, 2016). MV: €100 M

Ousmane Dembélé: €105 M
(Borussia Dortmund to FC Barcelona, August 25, 2017)

Antoine Griezmann: €120 M
(Atlético de Madrid to FC Barcelona, July 14, 2019)

Kylian Mbappé: €180 M
(Monaco to Paris Saint-Germain, August 31, 2017)

A €295.40 M SUBS BENCH

Alphonse Areola
(Paris Saint-Germain). MV: €17.5 M

Nabil Fekir: €19.75 M + €10 M bonus
(Olympique Lyon to Real Betis, July 23, 2019)

Olivier Giroud: €17 M
(Arsenal FC to Chelsea, January 31, 2018)

Presnel Kimpembe:
(Paris Saint-Germain). MV: €30 M

Thomas Lemar: €70 M
(Monaco to Atlético de Madrid, July 1, 2018)

Steve Mandanda: €3 M
(Crystal Palace to Olympique de Marseille, July 11, 2017)

Blaise Matuidi: €25 M
(Paris Saint-Germain to Juventus FC, August 18, 2017)

Benjamin Mendy: €57.50 M
(Monaco to Manchester City FC, July 24, 2017)

Steven Nzonzi: €26.65 M
(Sevilla FC to AS Roma, August 14, 2018)

Adil Rami: €3 M
(Marseille to Fenerbahçe, August 27, 2019)

Djibril Sidibé: €15 M
(Lille OSC to Monaco, July 8, 2016). €15 M

Florian Thauvin: €11 M
(Newcastle to Olympique de Marseille, July 1, 2017)

Note: for any player who has not been the object of a transfer since before the start of the 2016/2017 season, their market value (MV), as of September 3, 2019, has been indicated.

Source: Transfermarkt

KAZAN (RUSSIA), KAZAN ARENA
JUNE 16, 2018
Les Bleus congratulate themselves after
beating Australia 2–1 in their first match
of the 2018 FIFA World Cup.

MOSCOW (RUSSIA), LUZHNIKI STADIUM
JULY 15, 2018
Antoine Griezmann, Paul Pogba, and Kylian Mbappé (left to right)—all scorers in the World Cup final—show off the second star on their jerseys, following their victory over Croatia (4–2).

Uruguay

Four-star Celeste

TO URUGUAYAN EYES, THE PRESENCE OF FOUR STARS ON THE NATIONAL JERSEY SEEMS COMPLETELY NORMAL, DESPITE THE FACT THAT LA CELESTE HAS ONLY LIFTED TWO WORLD CUPS.

As is customary in football, each star symbolises a World Cup victory. This small South American nation, boasting a population of just 3.5 million, has two to its name (in 1930 and 1950). However, the reason that FIFA chose Uruguay as hosts for the first-ever World Cup in 1930 was due to their triumphs at consecutive Olympic Games, in 1924 and 1928, the only international football tournament in existence at the time. Uruguayans, therefore, regard this as akin to having won four World Cups. Copying Brazil, the first country to place stars on their jersey in 1970, Uruguay added four to its own in 2000. But FIFA amended their rules on April 1, 2010, stating that senior national teams should display a five-pointed star for each World Cup victory "on the front of the shirt at chest level, immediately adjacent to the Official Member Association Emblem" (Article 16, Chapter 4: Playing Equipment). Uruguay circumvented this new ruling by inserting the stars within the emblem, without placing any outside. La Celeste will therefore remain a four-star team for the foreseeable future.

4
GLOBAL HONOURS
2 FIFA World Cups
2 Olympic Games

15
CONTINENTAL HONOURS
15 Copas América

2011
Copa América–
winning jersey

1930
World Cup–
winning jersey

1950
World Cup–
winning jersey

1995
Copa América–
winning jersey

2002
Jersey worn
at World Cup

Cavani, Faith in his 21

As much as Edinson Cavani worships Gabriel Batistuta, the Argentinian number 9, to the point of emulating his long, flowing hair, he is more a devotee of Zinedine Zidane in regards to his choice of jersey number. The Frenchman may have played the number 10 position (attacking midfield playmaker) on the pitch, but he wore number 7 on his back at FC Girondins de Bordeaux (1992–96), followed by number 21 at Juventus (1996–2001). Cavani (El Matador) has regularly worn the number 9 since arriving at Paris SG in 2013, but he also wore the number 7 at US Palermo (2006–10) and at SCC Naples (2010–13). After starting out with the number 11, Cavani also wore the number 7 when he joined the national squad in 2008.

This choice was neither a happy coincidence nor the result of there being no other numbers available when Cavani began forging his professional career. It wasn't even a homage to Zidane. No, the reason is due to his deeply religious beliefs, since the number 7 in the Bible is synonymous with perfection. After all, six busy days of creation led to the plenitude of the seventh day. The number also evokes the seven sayings spoken by Jesus on the Cross, the seven trumpets of the Apocalypse, the seven Sacraments, the seven deadly sins, and the seven gifts of the Holy Spirit.

And although Cavani kept his number 7 at club level until his arrival in France, he soon abandoned it for the 21 when he joined the Uruguayan national side. This was a curious choice for a striker, but not for him. Ever fueled by his faith, this multiple of 7 evoked for him the number of quasi-divine protection. The number 21 is an indicator of chance, protection, success, and creative inspiration to rise higher in search of a certain plenitude. An expression of balance and harmony, 21 encourages success, dedication, and fulfillment. In short, 21 suits Cavani perfectly.

FORTALEZA (BRAZIL), ARENA CASTELÃO
JUNE 14, 2014, 24TH MINUTE
"This is crazy," Edinson Cavani seems to be saying, after scoring in his first World Cup match against Costa Rica (1–3).

United under the same colours

BEFORE BECOMING A MIGHTY WINNING MACHINE, SPAIN SUFFERED FOR MANY YEARS FROM THE RIVALRY BETWEEN THE CASTILIANS OF MADRID AND THE CATALANS OF BARCELONA.

Spanish football always produced great players, like Alfredo Di Stéfano, who was born in Argentina but played for Spain for most of his life, and won European Footballer of the Year in 1957 and 1959, and Luis Suárez, who won the same award in 1960. But for many years, *La Roja* (as the national team is known) was often relegated to a position of secondary importance in a country defined by regional differences. Undermined by the rivalry between Real Madrid—symbol of the establishment and centralised power—and Catalan representatives Barcelona, whose supporters were hostile to General Franco (1939–75), the Spaniards rarely played and won together. That changed with the appointment of Madrid-born Luis Aragonés to the helm of the national side in 2004. Taking advantage of an exceptional generation of players led by Iniesta and Xavi, he was able to persuade the Madrid and Barcelona stars to unite, with victory as their common goal. After winning Euro 2008, Aragonés made way for the former Real Madrid coach, Vicente del Bosque, who built on the foundations laid by his predecessor to lead Spain to further glory at the 2010 World Cup and Euro 2012, the first time any nation won three consecutive major international competitions.

2
GLOBAL HONOURS
1 FIFA World Cup
1 Olympic Games

3
CONTINENTAL HONOURS
3 UEFA European Football Championships

2012
European
Championship–
winning jersey

1950
Jersey worn
at World Cup

1964
European
Championship–
winning jersey

1984
European
Championship–
runners-up jersey

2010
World Cup–
winning jersey

Villa and Ramos: first-name basis

It was not until the 1996–97 season that UEFA required its clubs to print players' names and numbers on the back of their jerseys. Some players, rather than using their full surnames, opted to only display their first name, which was the case for David Villa (Sánchez), Spain's record goalscorer, and his Spanish international teammate Sergio Ramos (García). So as to distinguish himself from Mali's Mahamadou Diarra, who arrived three years before him at Real Madrid (in 2006), French midfielder Lassana Diarra went for the shortened "Lass." Others approached it differently—at the start of the 1996–97 campaign, 1991 European Footballer of the Year Jean-Pierre Papin had his initials JPP inserted above the 27 (2+7=9) on his Bordeaux shirt, since the number 9 was already taken. Waïti, Bordeaux's main sponsor, started offering the JPP jersey free with the purchase of several packs of fruit juice, but the French football authorities soon put a stop to the marketing initiative. To distinguish himself from his father, a former Mexico international (1983–94) nicknamed "Chicharo" (the pea) because of his green eyes, Javier Hernández went with "Chicharito" (the little pea) on his back. Sebastián Abreu, meanwhile, preferred his name to be preceded by "El loco" (the madman) on his jersey when he was at Brazilian outfit Botafogo. But Carlos Tevez's attempts to play at the 2010 World Cup as "Carlitos," the name he had sported while at Boca Juniors and Corinthians, were blocked by FIFA. "Kun" Agüero and Jonás Gutiérrez were met with the same intransigence. They had taken things just a little too far.

CAPE TOWN (SOUTH AFRICA), GREEN POINT STADIUM
JUNE 29, 2010
David Villa salutes the fans, having just scored against Portugal to propel Spain through to the quarterfinals of the World Cup.

In the name of the rose

IN ADDITION TO THE THREE LIONS, TAKEN FROM THE COAT OF ARMS OF RICHARD THE LIONHEART, THE ENGLAND JERSEY FEATURES TEN TUDOR ROSES TO SYMBOLISE THE UNITY ACHIEVED IN THE FIFTEENTH CENTURY.

In the forty-three years from 1966 to 2009, England changed their shirts forty-five times. However, they have worn the coat of arms of Richard the Lionheart since their first match, on November 30, 1872, against Scotland (0–0). Reigning as king between 1189 and 1199, Richard I was the epitome of chivalry and royalty, and his coat of arms took the form of three azure lions, one above the other. For the FA, the world's oldest football association (1863), "it was a powerful symbol raised by the throne of England during the Crusades and appropriated by a team heading into combat." To distinguish it from the crest of the cricket team, the FA added the floral emblem of England in 1949. This was a Tudor rose (red with a white centre), the symbol of the unification of the houses of Lancaster (red) and York (white) that occurred when the Tudor Henry VII married Elizabeth of York, putting an end to the War of the Roses (1455–85). While the coat of arms used by the England rugby team has only one rose, the football version has ten, one for each league within the FA (in 1949), displayed on a field of silver.

1
GLOBAL HONOUR
1 FIFA World Cup

0
CONTINENTAL HONOUR

1966
World Cup–
winning jersey

1872
Jersey worn during
the first international
football match

1930
Away jersey,
red since this date

1935
Royal blue jersey

2012
Jersey worn during
European
Championship

England

A tradition dies hard

England likes to stay true to its traditions, including in football. The eleven players who begin a game wear the numbers 1 through 11. So when a regular starter like Wayne Rooney is selected as a substitute, the number 10 he would normally wear is given to the player on the field.[*]

The first use of numbering in England dates back to August 25, 1928, when Arsenal and Chelsea both had numbers on their shirts when they played against The Wednesday (later renamed Sheffield Wednesday) and Swansea Town, respectively. The initiative did not continue. Following objections that adding numbers to the jerseys was not only too costly but also unattractive, the league's governing body rejected a proposal requiring numbered shirts.

As for the England national team, they played with numbers for the first time in a competitive match on April 17, 1937, against Scotland. The numbers were assigned based on the players' positions: 1 for the goalkeeper, 2 for the right-back, and so on in ascending order, up to the front, right to left, respecting the 2-3-5 formation, and ending with the number eleven, the left winger. The league finally followed suit on June 5, 1939. But with World War II beginning that year the change did not go into full effect until 1946.

The addition of players' names to jerseys happened much more recently. They first appeared on England shirts during Euro 1992, when UEFA made names mandatory. The Premier League then made names and assigning a number obligatory, starting from the 1993–1994 season.

ROME (ITALY), STADIO OLIMPICO
OCTOBER 11, 1997
The unforgettable image of Paul Ince's blood-soaked number 4 shirt during a qualifying match for the 1998 World Cup against Italy. FIFA now forces players to change their jerseys should they become bloodied.

(*)In some instances England cannot maintain this policy. Both FIFA and UEFA require players in the final stages of tournaments to keep their shirt number. But as can be seen in the qualifying games for the 2014 World Cup, England were assigned numbers on a match-by-match basis.

Mexico's nod to Aztec ancestors

DESPITE BEING DECIMATED BY SPANISH INVADERS, THE AZTECS ARE ALIVE AND WELL IN THE HEARTS OF MEXICANS, WHO HONOUR THEIR PREDECESSORS' FOUNDING MYTH ON THE NATIONAL FOOTBALL TEAM CREST.

Legend has it that the Mexica people, renamed Aztecs by the Spanish conquistadors, received an order from one of their gods, Huitzilopochtli, to abandon Aztlan and northern Mexico and settle wherever they found an eagle perched on a cactus, eating a serpent. Eight tribes marched for two hundred years, until one day the prophecy came true in the middle of the swamps. The travellers dried themselves off in 1325 and founded Tenochtitlán, which would eventually become the capital of a massive empire stretching from Texas to Honduras. The fall of Mexico on August 13, 1521 changed nothing. While large Spanish structures were built atop the spongy soil, the myth remained unshakable for many Mexicans, to the extent that it figures on the national flag and on the jersey worn by *El Tri*, the nickname given to their team in reference to the country's three national colours: green (for hope), white (for purity), and red (for the blood of heroes). When saluting the flag, every player places their right hand by the coat of arms, palm facing down, hoping that a sprinkling of Aztec magic will provide an extra advantage in the ninety-minute battle ahead.

2
GLOBAL HONOURS
1 FIFA Confederations Cup
1 Olympic Games

11
CONTINENTAL HONOURS
11 Gold Cups

2006
Jersey worn
at World Cup

1930
First jersey worn
at World Cup

1978
Away jersey worn
at World Cup

1994
Jersey worn
at World Cup

2019
Gold Cup–
winning jersey

Campos, Mexico's colour man

When he was not keeping goal for his country, Jorge Campos was scoring goals for his clubs. While the actual figures vary from one Mexican statistician to another, what is clear is that he netted at least thirty-five in a sixteen-year career, fourteen of those coming in just one season (1989–90) for Mexican side Pumas. Before Campos earned a reputation as a flying keeper, it was in the role of striker that he excelled while growing up in Acapulco, where he was born on October 15, 1966. But Campos's eccentric streak and taste for the spectacular did not end there. El Tri's legendary custodian also knew how to stand out from the crowd, appearing in some unique kits. During United States 1994, the first of his two World Cup experiences, he made a name for himself globally by wearing a fluorescent pink, green, yellow, and red jersey/shorts get-up. The whimsical Mexican got into the habit of coming up with the creative jersey designs himself. His impressive total of 130 caps, amassed between 1991 and November 10, 2004, makes Campos not only one the most colourful goalkeepers of all time, but one of Mexico's best between the posts.

Jorge Campos in some of the eccentric, self-designed goalkeeping jerseys that became his trademark.

Soviet style

BEFORE GAINING A CERTAIN RETRO CACHET, THE HAMMER-AND-SICKLE-STAMPED JERSEY DRAPED THE BACKS OF THE SOVIET UNION'S BEST FOOTBALLERS AS THEY TOOK ON THE WORLD.

The iconic red top with "CCCP"—the Cyrillic alphabet's equivalent of "USSR" (Union of Soviet Socialist Republics)—stamped across it was worn for the first time on August 21, 1923, in Stockholm, in a match against Sweden. For a long time, the Soviets were content to test themselves exclusively in the Olympic Games (they won gold in 1956 and 1988), but only when they were not boycotting (as in 1948 in London and 1984 in Los Angeles). They finally made their World Cup debut in 1958. Although the sport was used as political propaganda, the USSR triumphed in just one non-Olympic international tournament, Euro 1960. They lost in the final of three others (the European Championships of 1964, 1972, and 1988). The USSR jersey would be given its final outing on November 13, 1991, in Larnaca, where its wearers defeated Cyprus 3–0. The breakup of the Soviet Union on December 26, 1991 led to the emergence of 15 separate national sides. Russia is considered by FIFA to be USSR's successor, and has inherited those now-defunct teams' results and records. It was a strange decision considering that a majority of the USSR's players came from the other fourteen republics, such as Georgia and Ukraine.

2

GLOBAL HONOURS

2 Olympic Games

1

CONTINENTAL HONOUR

1 UEFA European Football Championship

1960
European
Championship–
winning jersey

1923
First jersey

1966
Jersey worn
at World Cup

1988
European
Championship–
runners-up jersey

1991
Last official jersey

Kiev, factory of champions

A dilapidated two-storey building—demolished to make room for a luxury hotel in 1998—at one time housed some of the gems of Soviet football. But those rising talents, surprisingly, did not belong to one of the powerful Moscow clubs. They were brought through the ranks in the utmost secrecy at Koncha-Zaspa, the training complex belonging to Dynamo Kiev that was founded in 1927 by the forerunners to the KGB. It was there, in a well-to-do suburb of Kiev, that Valeriy Lobanovskyi (1939–2002), known as "The Master," shaped the futures of many great players with an iron hand. Lev Yashin, the only goalkeeper to be named European Footballer of the Year (in 1963), is also the only Soviet winner of the prestigious award to not have been coached by the unsmiling Lobanovskyi. From 1973 to 1990, Lobanovskyi's team ruled over Soviet football, and even managed to transfer that success to the continental stage, defeating Hungarian side Ferencváros 3–0 to lift the European Cup Winners' Cup on May 14, 1975. They also won the same competition again in 1986. That time period saw Dynamo provide a majority of players to the USSR national team, with whom Lobanovskyi enjoyed three separate coaching spells. Two of his players captured the European Footballer of the Year award during his tenure at Dynamo: Oleg Blokhin (in 1975) and Igor Belanov (in 1986). After the fall of the Berlin Wall on November 9, 1989, he had a hand in the development of another future winner, Andriy Shevchenko, who received the accolade in 2004 while playing for AC Milan. The year before, Shevchenko laid his hands on the trophy that his mentor had always dreamed of holding: the Champions League.

LEFT TO RIGHT (TOP), AND LEFT TO RIGHT (BOTTOM)
Lev Yashin (the only goalkeeper ever named European Footballer of the Year), Oleg Blokhin (second Soviet player to win the award in 1975), Igor Belanov (1986 European Footballer of the Year), and Andrei Shevchenko (2004's winner).

Cameroon

Big ideas, short sleeves

IN 2002 AND 2004, THE INDOMITABLE LIONS WERE AS UNPREDICTABLE WITH THEIR CHOICE OF SHIRTS AS THEY WERE ON THE PITCH. AND THEIR FASHION FAUX PAS ATTRACTED THE WRATH OF FIFA.

In 2000, keen to provide Adidas and Nike with competition, Puma produced several innovative football kits. For Italy, they created a set of tight-fitting jerseys designed to put an end to shirt-pulling. Then at the 2002 African Cup of Nations, they designed sleeveless shirts for Cameroon. FIFA, worried about the lack of space on the sleeves for their logo, banned the top from the World Cup. So Puma added black sleeves. And at the 2004 African Cup of Nations, Puma made the bold move of kitting Cameroon out with their UniQT jersey, a skintight, one-piece outfit. FIFA banned the team from wearing it in the quarterfinals, which Cameroon lost. On April 16, 2004, Cameroon were fined €128,900 and had six points deducted from their 2006 World Cup qualifying campaign, before FIFA had a change of heart the very next month and lifted the penalty. FIFA's Law 4, defining the players' equipment, had been found wanting. And it would not be the last time: on July 5, 2012, FIFA, under pressure from the Asian Football Confederation, authorised the wearing of veils in women's tournaments.

1
GLOBAL HONOUR
1 Olympic Games

5
CONTINENTAL HONOURS
5 African Cups of Nations

2004
UniQt jersey, worn during the Africa Cup of Nations (skintight one-piece outfit)

1982
First jersey worn at World Cup

1990
Jersey worn at World Cup

2002
African Cup of Nations jersey vs. World Cup jersey

2017
African Cups of Nations–winning jersey

Milla: an African adventure

Roger Milla was not your average footballer. He was more of a dancer in football boots. He proved as much at the 1990 World Cup, where Milla was ordered to play by the president of Cameroon. Seventeen minutes after replacing Emmanuel Maboang, the old Indomitable Lion roared in triumph by beating Silviu Lung in the Romanian goal. Milla ran to the corner flag, placed his left hand on his stomach, raised his right hand to the heavens, and began to sway this way and that, inventing a dance that caught the attention of the watching world.

"I did it spontaneously. It wasn't planned out," he said. "It's not the Makossa, it's the Milla dance! It's a mix of all kinds of Cameroonian dances." Milla had launched a new craze, and ever since then, footballers have tried to imitate him.

Milla headed for the corner flag to dance again after scoring once more in the 86th minute to complete a 2–1 victory. And he scored twice more against Colombia in the first knockout round (in the 106th and 109th minutes of extra time). Thanks to Milla's goals, an African team were in the quarterfinals for the first time (where they would lose 3–2 to England after extra time). Milla returned for the 1994 World Cup, and one minute after replacing Louis-Paul M'Fédé against Russia on June 28, the fans in San Francisco were on their feet. Milla showed off his dancing skills in front of 75,000 spectators, scoring his team's only goal in a 6–1 defeat. But Cameroon were out. The old Lion retired having become the first African to play in three World Cups and the oldest player to play at and score in a World Cup (aged forty-two years and thirty-nine days).

NAPLES (ITALY), STADIO SAN PAOLO
JUNE 23, 1990
Roger Milla celebrates the first of his two goals against Colombia.

Japan

An ever-rising sun

MADE TO WAIT UNTIL 1988 TO MAKE THEIR FIRST APPEARANCE IN AN INTERNATIONAL TOURNAMENT, JAPAN IS NOW, ALONGSIDE SOUTH KOREA, THE MOST FORMIDABLE FOOTBALLING NATION IN ASIA.

In Japanese symbolism, the black crow, a figure of family love, is considered good luck. It heralded victory for the samurai and embodied their virtue. Thought to represent the sun, such as the one at the centre of the national flag, the bird's appearance in the empire's official records dates back to approximately 700 AD. The Japanese FA placed a three-legged crow at the heart of the team jersey's crest, its third foot clutching a red ball. But it took its time in bringing luck to the Land of the Rising Sun, as demonstrated by the results of their first two matches, 5–0 and 15–2 defeats to China and the Philippines, respectively, on the ninth and tenth of May 1917. The "Samurai Blue" (a neutral colour, with no association to the red and white of the imperial flag) did not actually qualify for an international competition until the Asian Cup of 1988. The launch of the J. League on May 15, 1993 then precipitated the arrival of high-profile foreign players (Bebeto, Lineker, Schillaci, and Stoichkov, among others) and managers (Ardiles, Littbarski, Arsène Wenger, and more). Reaching their first World Cup in 1998, Japan then qualified for the next five, reaching the quarterfinals in 2002, 2010, and 2018. The only nation to win the AFC Asia Cup four times, their players have truly established themselves at European clubs, and the women's team were crowned world champions in 2011, overcoming the United States on penalties after a 2–2 draw.

0

GLOBAL HONOUR

4

CONTINENTAL HONOURS
4 AFC Asian Cups

2011
Asian Cup–
winning jersey

1956
Jersey worn
at Olympic Games

1992
First Asian Cup–
winning jersey

1998
First jersey worn
at World Cup

2012
Home jersey

Nakata: what's in a name?

The convoy of buses making their way to each match at Perugia's Stadio Renato Curi would often seem endless. Throughout 1999 alone, thirty thousand football tourists made the long trip from Japan to profess their admiration for the new emperor, a man named Hidetoshi Nakata. The orange-haired midfielder was not, however, the first Japanese player to try his luck in Europe. But neither Yasuhiko Okudera, the first pioneer (in Germany, 1977–86), nor Kazu Miura, the first to play in Italy (with Genoa in 1994), shared his head for business. Upon his arrival at Roma, Nakata pocketed $1 million simply by selling a limited series of one thousand signed jerseys. As the owner of his own image rights via his Sunny Side Up management company, Nakata, who became interested in football after watching the long-running animated football programme *Captain Tsubusa* when he was a boy, also sold his image to a manga comic, a brand of saké, a video game, and more. Perugia would not regret shelling out €2.4 million to Hiratsuka-based club Shonan Bellmare for Nakata in 1998. They sold the creative midfield man to Roma in 2000 for €21.7 million, and the Romans transferred him on to Parma for €30.5 million the following year. Nakata's status as the most expensive Asian in football history is due in part to the fact that, like David Beckham, he was one of the first players to create a link between sport and fashion. In 2000, his name sold more jerseys than any other star save Ronaldo, and in 2004, he earned the same amount as the Brazilian (€16 million). Only Beckham (€30 million) and Zinedine Zidane (€19 million) were bringing in more at the time. He retired early on July 3, 2006, at just twenty-nine, in order to travel. But his business sense never left him. On March 30, 2011, a Taiwanese actress paid 27.6 million yen to purchase a pair of Nakata's signed boots at auction.

NANTES (FRANCE), STADE DE LA BEAUJOIRE
JUNE 20, 1998
Hidetoshi Nakata in action against Croatia in Japan's first World Cup, where they finished last in Group H.

Portugal

At Christ's orders

THE IMPOSING COAT OF ARMS OVER THE PLAYERS' HEARTS SAYS MUCH ABOUT THE RICH PAST OF THIS LITTLE EUROPEAN COUNTRY AND THE FERVENT CATHOLIC FAITH OF ITS TEN MILLION INHABITANTS.

The coat of arms is placed over the heart and takes up a large space on the Portugal team's shirt. In itself, it sums up the history of Portugal. First of all, the cross pattée derives from the Military Order of Christ, a religious order that was involved in the founding of the kingdom of Portugal in the twelfth century and played a significant role in its extraordinary maritime expansion. (Indeed, this famous cross appeared on the white sails of the Portuguese caravels.) In the centre are five blue shields on a white background, from which comes the nickname Seleção das Quinas (Team of the Set of Five). They symbolise the victory over the five Moorish kings at the Battle of Ourique, on July 25, 1139, which enabled the proclamation of the first king of Portugal. The five white spots on each shield represent the five wounds of Christ on the Cross. The shields also appear on the Portuguese flag, from which derive the green and red used as colours for the national team's home kit. When playing away, the Seleção sometimes wear white and blue, the colours of the kingdom of Portugal, although it has on occasion played in black (2013) and in green (2016).

0
GLOBAL HONOUR

2
CONTINENTAL HONOURS
1 UEFA European Football Championship
1 UEFA Nations League

2016
European
Championship–
winning jersey

1966
Jersey worn
at World Cup (match
for the third place)

2000
Jersey worn
at European
Championship

2004
European
Championship–
runners-up jersey

2019
UEFA Nations
League–
winning jersey

CR7ᵗʰ heaven

Cristiano Ronaldo looked set to experience a disastrous night on July 10, 2016. By the end it was one of the most beautiful moments of his life. As he was stretchered off the pitch in the twenty-fifth minute of the Euro 2016 final, it seemed as if his dreams of succeeding where the great Eusebio da Silva Ferreira had failed in the 1966 World Cup—when Portugal placed third—had vanished, and that his national team would not win their first trophy. But this would have been to underestimate such a true competitor. Returning to the bench with his thigh bandaged, he took on the role of a manager and supported his team from the sidelines. Once again, he found himself in the spotlight, even though he wasn't playing. Ronaldo's active presence on the bench helped to disconcert the French, who were defeated by a goal from Éder (Éderzito Lopes) in the 109ᵗʰ minute (1–0 in extra time).

When Cristiano Ronaldo left the Stade de France, he felt as if he were in seventh heaven. "CR7" has become the eternal brand of an exceptional champion who drove his team to victory. A brand that, according to a 2017 estimate by the Portuguese Institute of Marketing Administration (IPAM), was worth €102 million. And Ronaldo is keen to preserve and develop it. After starting his career at Sporting Lisbon in 2002 with number 28 on his back, number 7 soon became permanently glued to his initials. Except for when he moved to Real Madrid in 2009, where this number belonged to Raúl González Blanco. Upon the local star's departure for FC Schalke 04 one year later, Ronaldo dropped the 9 and took "his" 7 back.

Ronaldo has taken the CR7 name and made it famous in the most unlikely of arenas: the branding of his own line of underwear. He opened his first CR7 underwear store in Funchal, Portugal. Since then, the man with the perfect abs has extended his clothing line to include jeans, shoes, and accessories. On December 11, 2015, the new striker for Juventus FC (where Juan Cuadrado had been kindly asked to relinquish his number 7) partnered with the Portuguese Pestana Hotel Group to open six CR7 branded hotels by 2021.

SAINT-DENIS (FRANCE), STADE DE FRANCE
JULY 10, 2016
Cristiano Ronaldo, captain of Portugal, lifts the Henri Delaunay Trophy after beating France in the final of the UEFA European Football Championship (1–0 in extra time).

The Netherlands

Not-so-clockwork orange

BIRTHPLACE OF "TOTAL FOOTBALL," THE NETHERLANDS HAVE APPEARED IN THREE WORLD CUP FINALS, LOSING EACH TIME.

The Netherlands have historically worn their iconic orange jersey, black shorts, and orange socks with pride and panache. The black and orange harken back to the coat of arms of William of Orange, who achieved independence for the United Provinces. But one of the team's nicknames, "Clockwork Orange," stems more from the renowned "Total Football" they perfected than the colours on their backs. Over the years, however, things have not always gone like clockwork for the Flying Dutchmen. Although they secured their one and only European Championship title in 1988 (2–0 vs. USSR, June 25), they were defeated in every one of the three World Cup finals they played in, including two in a row against the host nation in the 1970s (1–2 vs. West Germany in 1974; 1–3 aet vs. Argentina in 1978; and 0–1 aet vs. Spain in 2010, in South Africa). Only Germany/West Germany have lost more often (four times), but they, at least, also have four triumphs to their name. Thirteen different teams have reached the World Cup final through the years, and the Oranje are one of just five of them—alongside Hungary, Czechoslovakia (two finals each), Croatia, and Sweden (one appearance each)—to have never lifted the trophy.

0

GLOBAL HONOUR

1

CONTINENTAL HONOUR

1 UEFA European Football Championship

2010
World Cup–
runners-up jersey

1950
First jersey

1974
World Cup–
runners-up jersey

1978
World Cup–
runners-up jersey

1988
European
Championship–
winning jersey

Depay, designated survivor

Wesley Sneijder retired from international football on the evening of his one hundred and thirty-fourth selection (a Dutch record) to the cheers of the crowd at the Johan-Cruyff ArenA, on September 6, 2018. As he stepped off the pitch in Amsterdam, in the sixty-second minute of a friendly match against Peru (2–1), he made one final, powerful gesture: "I symbolically hand over my jersey number [10] to [Memphis] Depay [scorer of the two winning goals]. He got my final Dutch jersey. He showed everyone how good he is at the moment. I hope he continues this way. We gonna enjoy him in the Dutch team." With this act, the man who came fourth in the 2010 Ballon d'Or passed on a message: at the age of twenty-four, it's time that Depay asserts his leadership over the new generation of Dutch players, and particularly those of Ajax Amsterdam, the surprise semifinalist of the Champions League a few months later (1–0, 2–3 against Tottenham, on April 30 and May 8, 2019, respectively).

Up until then, in both his club and international career, Depay had never worn the number 10, having preferred 22, 11, and above all the legendary number 7, which he wore at Manchester United for two seasons (2015–17), a time when the specialist online sports retailer Kitbag ranked Depay's shirt as 2015's third biggest seller, behind Lionel Messi and Cristiano Ronaldo. But ever since that September 2018 evening, he has worn number 10 for international games. "Since I joined the national team, [Wesley] took me under his wing. . . . [He] was a big inspiration for me. [That he gave me his shirt and his number 10] is a wonderful compliment, so I'm glad to take it." Now it's up to him to prove himself worthy of this legacy.

HAMBURG (GERMANY), VOLKSPARKSTADION
SEPTEMBER 6, 2019
Ever since Wesley Sneijder's retirement from international football in 2018, Memphis Depay has worn number 10 for the Netherlands, as seen here when they beat Germany 4–2 in the qualifying stage for Euro 2020.

Croatia

When the Vatreni inspired Barça

ON JUNE 3, 2019, THE WORLD CUP RUNNERS-UP WERE GREATLY SURPRISED TO DISCOVER THAT FC BARCELONA HAD RIPPED OFF THEIR FAMOUS CHECKERBOARD KIT, THE SYMBOL OF THIS YOUNG COUNTRY.

The Croatian international Ivan Rakitić has felt much less homesick at Barça since the 2019–20 season. Having featured vertical blue-and-garnet stripes on its kit for 120 years, Barça caused a stir in 2015, when it switched to horizontal stripes. But this was nothing compared to the surprise of June 3, 2019, when the club made a clean break with its traditional stripes by officially unveiling its new jersey . . . featuring a checkerboard design! Nike, Barça's kit supplier since 1998 (when Croatia finished third in the World Cup), justified this historic change by claiming it was a homage to the residential blocks laid out on a grid pattern so typical of the Catalan city. But the *Vatreni* (the Fiery Ones) didn't believe a word of it. Neither did the Croatian Football Federation (HNS). In a swiftly posted tweet, they cheekily referenced Barça's rip-off of the young country's emblematic checkerboard shirt: "Nice try @FCBarcelona, but you can't beat red-and-white checkers" and followed up with "Well, we are convinced that @ivanrakitic will surely enjoy the new @FCBarcelona kit!"

2020
FC Barcelona
home jersey

0
GLOBAL
HONOUR

0
CONTINENTAL
HONOUR

2018
World Cup–
runners-up jersey

1991
First jersey worn
after independence

1996
Jersey worn during
first international
competition

1998
Jersey worn
at World Cup (match
for third place)

2016
Jersey worn during
European
Championship

Modrić, from 14 to Number 1

On December 3, 2018, Luka Modrić stepped forward onto the balcony of the Grand Palais in Paris as number one. In the absence of Cristiano Ronaldo and Lionel Messi—winners of the last ten Ballon d'Or (five each)—not to mention Neymar, who skipped the ceremony in favor of playing *Call of Duty* (streamed on Twitch) with his compatriots Marquinhos and Thiago Silva, the captain of Croatia saw his immense talent finally rewarded. Winner of the UEFA Champions League with Real Madrid six months earlier (3–1 against Liverpool), and finalist of a World Cup in which he was voted best player, Modrić lifted the sixty-third Ballon d'Or.

Aged thirty-four, Modrić joins his idol Johan Cruyff (triple winner: 1971, 1973, and 1974) in this footballers' pantheon. Indeed, when he began his international career in 2006, Modrić wore the number 14 shirt in homage to "the Flying Dutchman," and he kept it for the next three years. Later, at Tottenham Hotspur, he refused to wear the prestigious number 10, despite being the perfect playmaker. No, Modrić would keep number 14 throughout his four years in the Premier League.

But when Modrić arrived at Real, in 2012, he could no longer allow himself to keep the number of Cruyff, who had played such a key role at Barça, the Madrid club's historic rival. So Modrić fell back on number 19 for five years. When the Colombian player James Rodriguez left for Bayern Munich in 2017, the number 10 became free, and Modrić naturally took it. Yet switching from 14 to 10 changed nothing about his extraordinary technique and tactical vision, which enabled him to become the first player of the former Yugoslavia, and the first Croatian, to receive the Ballon d'Or (Davor Šuker had finished second, behind Zinedine Zidane, in 1998). Modrić is quite simply the top footballer on the planet.

MOSCOW (RUSSIA), LUZHNIKI STADIUM
JULY 15, 2018
Luka Modrić, Croatia's captain and number 10 during the 2018 World Cup final (2-4 against France).

Football's first ladies

IN THE UNITED STATES, THE WOMEN'S NATIONAL TEAM HAS ACHIEVED A LEVEL OF POPULARITY AND NOTORIETY RARELY SEEN IN OTHER COUNTRIES. THEY ARE THE ONLY FEMALE NATIONAL SIDE TO WEAR FOUR STARS ON THEIR JERSEY.

After the collapse of the NASL, soccer appeared to have had its day in the United States. But the success of women's soccer and the start of a new men's professional league—Major League Soccer—in 1996 helped the sport survive and grow. Now, almost thirty years after the end of the NASL, soccer is thriving and has become an important part of the sporting landscape in the US. Six years after the US Women played their first match on August 18, 1985 (a 1–0 loss to Italy), the team, inspired by Michelle Akers, triumphed in the inaugural 1991 Women's World Cup in China. Since then, the Americans have never finished lower than third in the FIFA tournament, and they have secured four Olympic titles. The success of the 1994 Men's World Cup helped launch MLS, and the league has grown to include nineteen teams. The fan support has steadily improved over the years, and MLS is now ranked seventh in attendance for all leagues around the world. Although the American women have had the misfortune of witnessing two professional leagues fold, a third, which is being run by the US Soccer Federation and called the National Women's Soccer League (NWSL), began in the spring of 2013. With a new business model and the main goal of sustainability, the league's aim is to help the women's game develop even more in the US. The hope is that Team United States will remain on top of the world—after all, they are the only nation to wear four stars on their jersey (1991, 1999, 2015, 2019).

8

GLOBAL HONOURS

4 FIFA Women's World Cups
4 Olympic Games

8

CONTINENTAL HONOURS

8 Gold Cups

2019
World Cup–
winning jersey

1991
First World Cup–
winning jersey

1996
First Olympic gold
medal–winning jersey

2011
World Cup–
runners-up jersey

2012
Olympic Games–
winning jersey

United States

Women and the beautiful game

Women have played football for almost as long as men, and the women's game has attracted audiences that rival the men's. Indeed, in England, the popularity of women's football in the early twentieth century was so great that some say it jeopardized its own future.

One game in particular was pivotal in the history of the women's game. On December 26, 1920, 53,000 fans attended a match at Goodison Park (home to Everton FC), featuring Dick, Kerr's Ladies FC, named after a munitions factory where women worked during World War I. Records indicate that even more fans tried to see the game but were turned away. Within one year women's teams were banned from all FA affiliated grounds. Some players and press have speculated that the decision was made in an effort to keep audiences focused on the men's game.

The ban wasn't lifted until 1969, the same year that the famed Doncaster Belles were founded by lottery ticket sellers at Belle Vue stadium, the home of Doncaster Rovers FC. The Belles went on to dominate the sport in England, winning six FA Women's Cups and reaching the final on a further seven occasions. Women's football was embraced in other countries, notably within Scandinavia and the US, especially during the second half of the twentieth century. Colleges and universities fostered the sport, and it flourished in the 1980s with the celebrated North Carolina university team who won 21 of the first 31 women's National Collegiate Athletics Association (NCAA) titles.

One of the iconic images of the 1990s is of the US defender Brandi Chastain jubilant after scoring the decisive penalty against China in the final of the 1999 World Cup (0–0, 5–4 on penalties, July 10). She graced the covers of numerous prestigious publications, such as *Time*, *Newsweek*, and *Sports Illustrated*, propelling the women's game into the limelight once more.

LEFT TO RIGHT (TOP), AND LEFT TO RIGHT (BOTTOM)
North Carolina forward Mia Hamm at Fetzer Field, Chapel Hill, North Carolina (1993); Leonie Maier of Germany (2nd in FIFA's world rankings behind the US) and Shinobu Ohno of Japan (ranked 3rd) during an international friendly at the Allianz Arena in Munich, Germany (June 29, 2013); US defender Brandi Chastain on the cover of *Sports Illustrated* (July, 1999); Megan Rapinoe proudly displays the trophy following the United States's fourth World Cup title, in 2019.

Why Brandi Chastain and the U.S. Women's
Soccer Team Were Unbeatable

Regal roots

NAMED "CLUB OF THE CENTURY" BY FIFA IN 2000, REAL MADRID, OFFICIALLY FOUNDED ON MARCH 6, 1902, DID NOT ORIGINALLY PLAY IN THE NOW FAMOUS ALL-WHITE STRIP.

A blue diagonal stripe, like the one on their crest, appeared across the Spanish club's jerseys in the early days. Captivated by the elegance of London-based side Corinthians, who played in white shirts and trousers, the Real management decided to change to all white. After becoming known as *Los Merengues*, they added buttons, as well as the club crest (which remains there to this day) at chest level. The "White House" received royal patronage and became Real Madrid Club de Fútbol in 1920, and the crown of Alfonso XIII was added to the top of their crest. It was replaced in 1931 by a blue band, representing the region of Castile, upon the establishment of the Second Republic. Madrid regained its *Real Corona* (royal crown) in 1941, two years after the end of the Spanish Civil War. So as to avoid offending the United Arab Emirates, with whom they agreed to open an island theme park in 2015, the club removed the Catholic cross from the crown in their crest in 2012.

26
GLOBAL HONOURS
13 UEFA Champions Leagues
2 UEFA Europa Leagues
4 UEFA Super Cup
7 Intercontinental Cups

62
NATIONAL HONOURS
33 Spanish Leagues
19 Spanish Cups
10 Spanish Super Cups

2014
Spanish League–
winning jersey

1933
Spanish League–
winning jersey

1956-60
5 times in a row
Champions League–
winning jersey

1987
Spanish League–
winning jersey *(Quinta
del Buitre* period)

2000
Champions League–
winning jersey

Real Madrid

Zidane, a Legendary 5

Zinedine Zidane may well go down in history as an exceptional number 10—in the vein of Pelé, Diego Maradona, Lionel Messi, Michel Platini, and Zico (Arthur Antunes Coimbra)—yet it was really the number 5 that suited him to a tee. When he arrived in Madrid, on July 9, 2001, the number 10 already belonged to Luis Figo. With the 7 belonging to Raúl, the 8 to Steve McManaman, the 9 to Morientes, and the 11 to Sávio Bortolini Pimentel, the Frenchman fell back on number 5—usually allocated to a player occupying a defensive role—which had become free following the retirement of Manuel Sanchís. And Zidane kept it till 2006, right to the end of his playing days.

That number 5 had always brought him glory—to such an extent that, rather like Cristiano Ronaldo's 7, the number 5 is now a part of Zidane's image. Indeed, he has used this "registered trademark" to promote his sports complex in Aix-en-Provence, not far from his birthplace of Marseille, where five-a-side football is played.

In January 2016, Zidane replaced Rafael Benítez as manager of Real Madrid, and "five" took on a new resonance; in the space of a year, he pulled off a masterful five victories: La Liga, Spanish Super Cup, Champions League, UEFA Super Cup, and FIFA Club World Cup. Only the Copa del Rey escaped his clutches—taken by Barça. When his Real won a third consecutive Champions League in 2018, Zidane became the first manager to pull off such a feat since 1955, when the competition began—and all this in just two and a half years as manager. More than ever, Zidane is writing the history of football.

KIEV (UKRAINE), NATIONAL SPORTS COMPLEX OLIMPIYSKIY
MAY 26, 2018
Zidane has the right numbers.
When Real Madrid beat Liverpool 3–1 in the final of the UEFA Champions League, Zinedine Zidane became the first manager in history to win three Champions Leagues in a row.

Barça: More than a club

FORMED IN 1899, FC BARCELONA EMBODIES A DEEP-ROOTED CATALAN IDENTITY IN SPAIN, UNLIKE THEIR ETERNAL RIVALS FROM THE CAPITAL, REAL MADRID.

The eleven men—six Catalans, two Englishmen, two Swiss and a German—who responded to an advertisement in *Los Deportes* on October 22, 1899 had no way of realising that they were in the process of founding what would become one of the most powerful clubs in the world. The *blaugrana* colours (blue and dark red) were adopted the same year, ahead of a match against Català. And while their crest, shaped like a bowl from 1910 onwards, was the subject of various minor amendments up to 2002, it still takes its inspiration from the coat of arms of the city of Barcelona, which features the St. George's Cross alongside the Catalan flag.

Barça has always conveyed a strong Catalan identity, opposing the centralism of Madrid, to the extent that the club was closed for six months after the Spanish national anthem ("Marcha Real") was booed and whistled at on June 14, 1925. On August 6, 1936, a month after the start of the Spanish Civil War, then club president Josep Suñol, a Republican and Catalan nationalist, was arrested by forces loyal to General Franco and shot on the spot. Today, Barcelona remains a club that is anchored in its traditions yet still exudes a fearsome modernity.

20

GLOBAL HONOURS
5 UEFA Champions Leagues
3 UEFA Fairs Cups
4 UEFA Cup Winners' Cups
5 UEFA Super Cups
3 FIFA Club World Cups

69

NATIONAL HONOURS
26 Spanish Leagues
30 Spanish Cups
13 Spanish Super Cups

2015
Champions League–winning jersey

1903
First jersey

1979
First European trophy–winning jersey (the Cup Winners' Cup)

1992
First Champions League–winning jersey

1999
Centenary jersey

FC Barcelona

"Más que una camiseta" (*)

(*)More than a jersey

The *blaugrana* jersey had never featured a single advertisement until September 2006, when, for the first time in 107 years of existence, Barcelona struck up an ethical and humanitarian partnership with Unicef, agreeing to display the child-focused organisation's logo on the front of their jerseys. Barcelona even went as far as to donate €1.5 million per year to the United Nations programme, the first time such an arrangement had been considered in football. This was followed by another first, five years down the line, when Barça decided to place a sponsor on their shirts. Offering up to €170 million over six years, or nearly €30 million per season, the Qatar Foundation duly became the club's first official jersey sponsor. However, the contract included a clause enabling Qatar Sports Investments (QSI) to change the brand to be advertised. In line with this, QSI chose to feature Qatar Airways from the start of season 2013–14; 2014 was also the year in which Doha was scheduled to open its new international airport, predicted to become the second biggest in the world. In 2017, Barça opted for the Japanese e-commerce company Rakuten, which had a more neutral image than Qatar. Unicef remained on the back of the jersey, and with Rakuten on the front, Barça hoped to better penetrate the Asian market. The Catalans' shirt has become more than a jersey—it is now the symbol of a global club with 350 million supporters worldwide, as well as one of the most sold team shirts on the planet.

After a hundred and seven years of history, Lionel Messi's club introduced the advertisement on his shirt in 2006.

Boca Juniors

"La mitad màs uno"[*]

FOUNDED BY FACTORY WORKERS, LOS BOSTEROS (THE BUMPKINS) STATE PROUDLY THAT THEY ARE SUPPORTED BY OVER HALF OF ALL FOOTBALL FANS IN ARGENTINA.

The Genoese immigrants who established the Buenos Aires club on April 3, 1905 kept things simple—they gave it the name of the port district, La Boca, and added the word "Juniors" as a tribute to football's British roots. Realising that none of the colours they chose (pink, sky blue, or Juventus-style black-and-white stripes) were suitable, one of them suggested two years later that the club adopt the colours of the next boat that sailed into port. That boat happened to be Swedish, and Boca Juniors's now revered blue and yellow (originally a diagonal yellow stripe, but changed to a horizontal one in 1913) was born. When Mauricio Macri added two white stripes above and below the yellow band upon becoming club president in 1996, Diego Maradona himself threatened to stop wearing the jersey, before later changing his mind. Coca-Cola was forced to follow suit when *Los Xeneizes* ("The Genoese") asked the company to change the colour of the world-famous logo if it wanted to succeed Pepsi as jersey sponsor in 2004. The reason? Red and white are the colours of River Plate, the club's eternal rivals. Boca's stadium, known as "La Bombonera," thereby became the only place in the world where Coca-Cola's logo is black and white.

18
GLOBAL HONOURS
6 Copas Libertadores
1 Supercopa Libertadores
4 Recopas Sudamericana
2 Copas Sudamericana
1 Copa de Oro
1 Copa Master de Supercopa
3 FIFA Club World Cups

36
NATIONAL HONOURS
33 Argentinian Leagues
3 Argentinian Cups

2003
Argentinian League–, Copa Liberatores–, and FIFA Club World Cup–winning jersey

1905
First jersey

1907-12
Blue jersey with a diagonal yellow stripe

1913
Blue jersey with an horizontal yellow stripe

1996
Last jersey worn by Maradona

Boca Juniors

Riquelme, and the disputed succession

A former Boca star (1981–82 and 1995–97), Diego Maradona continues to support the club closest to his heart from the balcony of his private box.

Juan Román Riquelme could not have dreamed of a greater public tribute than the one he got on November 10, 2001, a day earmarked for celebrating the talents of Diego Maradona. Following a gala match organised in his honour at La Bombonera, "El Diez" took off his Argentina jersey to reveal the Boca Juniors equivalent, with number 10 and the name of the man he considered to be his rightful successor printed on its back: Riquelme. Four years earlier, on October 26, 1997, the cultured midfielder, a product of Argentinos Juniors's youth system like Maradona, had already replaced his idol at halftime of a 2–1 Superclásico away win over River Plate, Maradona's last official match in Boca colours. He proudly took on his hero's number 10 jersey for six months, before packing his bags for Barcelona, although it was at Villarreal (2003–07) that he would eventually rise to European prominence. Despite earning fifty-one caps and scoring seventeen goals for Argentina between 1997 and 2008, he never managed to truly fill Maradona's boots, however, even going so far as to quit international football after the 2006 World Cup. Alfio Basile, the new Argentinian coach, persuaded Riquelme to come out of retirement to play a part in beating Chile (2–0) on October 13, 2007, but definitively shut the door on La Albiceleste in March 2009, enraged after being ignored by Basile's successor. The coach in question, who refused to call up the skilful midfield man between October 28, 2008 and the 2010 World Cup, was none other than Maradona! "Riquelme is too slow," he claimed. "El Ultimo Numero Diez," as Riquelme was known, and who had a statue at La Bombonera erected in his honour on July 2, 2011, did gain some semblance of revenge on El Diez. In 2008, Riquelme was named Most Popular Player in Boca's History by fans, receiving 33.37% of the vote compared to Maradona's 26.42%. Riquelme was, perhaps, the rightful successor after all.

Juan Riquelme, seen here battling with River Plate captain Marcelo Gallardo, was named Most Popular Player in Boca's History by the club's fans in 2008.

AC Milan

"Il club piu titolato al mondo"[(*)]

(*)The most successful club in the world

TWENTY-ONE YEARS AFTER SAVING AC MILAN FROM BANKRUPTCY, SILVIO BERLUSCONI SAW HIS GRAND DREAMS COME TRUE IN 2007 AS THE CLUB BECAME THE MOST TROPHY-RICH TEAM IN THE WORLD.

"Il club piu titolato al mondo." Following the FIFA Club World Cup final on December 16, 2007, those six words were embroidered in gold on AC Milan's jersey, under the crest. This eighteenth international title propelled the club above Boca Juniors, the Argentinians they just defeated 4–2, meaning Milan had the most continental and global trophies among all the teams of the world. In addition, it represented the realisation of a long-held dream for Silvio Berlusconi, who had bought the then financially troubled outfit on February 20, 1986. It was a curious fate for a football and cricket (up till 1905) club founded on December 16, 1899 by ten Englishmen and seven Italians, whose first president, Herbert Kilpin, was a British vice-consul. Following the English trend at the time, the red-and-black striped jersey was adopted from the outset. Red for the devil and black to instil fear. They have not always been fearsome, and even less so since 2014 and the new world domination of Real, now the most successful club on the planet, with twenty-six titles.

18
GLOBAL HONOURS
7 UEFA Champions Leagues
2 UEFA Cup Winners' Cups
5 UEFA Super Cups
4 FIFA Club World Cup

30
NATIONAL HONOURS
18 Italian Leagues
5 Italian Cups
7 Italian Super Cups

1990
UEFA Super Cup–
winning jersey

1963
Champions League–
winning jersey

1969
Champions League–
winning jersey

2003
Home jersey

2007
Champions League–
winning jersey

AC Milan

Maldini's Turkish turmoil

The encounter was not planned. And it nearly turned into a riot. As soon as the AC Milan fans caught sight of their players entering Istanbul's international airport, they set about viciously insulting them, venting fury at their heroes' collapse in the UEFA Champions League final against Liverpool the night before, a match "I Rossoneri" lost on penalties after leading 3–0 at the break (May 25, 2005). But rather than follow the lead of his teammates who were rushing to get as far away as possible, Paolo Maldini stopped. He turned around, put his bag down, and made his way—alone—towards the volatile crowd of supporters. With a piercing glare, he looked right into their eyes and proclaimed: "You are the ones bringing shame on Milan!" The *capitano*, who opened the scoring versus the Reds just a few hours before, spoke at length to the fans, and calm soon reigned. Those fans would not forget the incident or other similar incidents, however. Contrary to Franco Baresi, the previous talismanic Milan captain, Maldini never enjoyed the support of the Ultras in the Curva Sud. Holding the opinion that defending the jersey with red-and-black stripes was the same as defending a certain sporting ethic, the Italian international constantly denounced the violence in which certain football supporters indulged, particularly those who followed his own team. The Ultras had their revenge some four years later, whistling at Maldini and displaying banners with hostile messages as he bid farewell to San Siro stadium. After swearing loyalty to a single jersey for the entirety of his twenty-five-year career, Maldini, a model professional, retired without the respect of a certain section of AC Milan's supporters; a club to which he nevertheless returned, on August 5, 2018, as director of sporting strategy and development, before being promoted to technical director ten months later.

YOKOHAMA (JAPAN), NISSAN STADIUM,
DECEMBER 16, 2007
AC Milan captain Paolo Maldini raises the club's eighteenth international trophy after helping overcome Boca Juniors in the final of the Club World Cup.

Liverpool

"You'll never walk alone"

BEING PART OF THE RED ARMY, AS LIVERPOOL'S SUPPORTERS ARE KNOWN, IS A GUARANTEE OF NEVER HAVING TO WALK ALONE, AS EXPRESSED BY THE ANTHEM AND MOTTO OF THE MERSEYSIDE CLUB, FOUNDED IN 1892.

Players that pull on a Liverpool jersey are aware that they carry a heavy burden. They must honour the memory of the victims of the Heysel Stadium disaster, where 39 supporters died after fences and a retaining wall collapsed on May 29, 1985, and of the Hillsborough disaster, when ninety-six fans perished following a crush on standing terraces on April 15, 1989.

Liverpool waited until 1896 to drop the blue and white sported by neighbours Everton and adopt a red jersey. The image of a liver bird, a mythical creature—half cormorant, half eagle—used to represent the city of Liverpool, was added to the jersey in 1955, and then to the badge in 1987. The twin flames on either side symbolise the Hillsborough memorial outside Anfield. Since 1992, the club motto—"you'll never walk alone"—has appeared above the shield surrounding the liver bird.

14

GLOBAL HONOURS

6 UEFA Champions Leagues
3 UEFA Europa Leagues
4 UEFA Super Cups
1 FIFA Club World Cup

48

NATIONAL HONOURS

18 English Leagues
7 FA Cups
8 English League Cups
15 Charity/Community Shields

2019
Champions League–
winning jersey

1892
First jersey

1896
First red jersey

1973
Europa League–
winning jersey

2005
Champions League–
winning jersey

Hot Numbers

When Mohamed Salah signed with Liverpool FC on June 22, 2017, he didn't realise that this would provide a boon for the Royal Mail. You see, when the Egyptian player arrived at his new club, he insisted on retaining the number 11, with which he had launched his career over the two previous seasons at AS Roma. The problem was that Roberto Firmino had already been wearing this number for the past two years. Firmino's latest official jersey, bearing the famous 11, had already gone on sale to Liverpool fans in advance of the next season. Anxious to please a player they had just bought for €42 million on a five-year contract, the Reds asked Firmino to give up his lucky number. Firmino agreed, much to the joy of his new teammate. "I appreciate what Firmino did. I have to thank him very much. I like the number 11; it was my number in Rome and also the national team before," explained Salah.

But the club asked Firmino for another favour: to personally sign every shirt already sold with "Firmino 11" printed on it. Ever the gentleman, the Brazilian agreed. Although fans could not get their money back, they had until August 18, 2017 to send their shirts to Anfield "with a stamped self-addressed envelope big enough to contain [the] jersey. It will then be signed by Firmino and returned … ," announced the club.

In return, Firmino inherited the prestigious number 9, previously worn by legends of the Reds such as Ian Rush (1980–87, 1988–96) and Robbie Fowler (1995–2002, 2006–07). As for the Senegalese left-winger Sadio Mané, he swapped his 19 for the 10 in 2018—a number that does not hold the same legendary weight at Liverpool as it does at many other clubs. And it would be thanks to these three numbers (9, 10, and 11) that Liverpool won the sixth Champions League title in their rich history, against Tottenham, on June 1, 2019 (2–0).

LIVERPOOL (ENGLAND), ANFIELD
AUGUST 23, 2017
Mohamed Salah, scorer against Hoffenheim in the home leg of the Champions League (4–2; away: 2–1), is congratulated by Sadio Mané.

From the gym to FC Hollywood

CREATED AFTER SPLITTING FROM A MULTI-SPORT ORGANISATION, BAYERN MUNICH HAVE BECOME, IN SPITE OF NUMEROUS INTERNAL PROBLEMS, ONE OF THE MOST WELL-SUPPORTED AND POWERFUL CLUBS IN EUROPE.

On the morning of February 27, 1900, the Munich gymnastics club of MTV 1879 refused to allow its football section to join the German FA (DFB). That very evening, eleven of its members founded FC Bayern Munich (*bayern* being the German word for "Bavarian"). However, the rise to power of the Nazis in 1933 brought their gradual development to an abrupt halt. Their president and coach, both Jewish, were forced to flee Germany, while Bayern, now referred to as the "Jewish club," battled against ignorance at home. It took them until 1965 to obtain promotion to the Bundesliga, two years after the launch of the professional championship. Despite several high-profile dramas that led to them gaining the nickname "FC Hollywood," the Bavarians have since become one of the most respected, stable, and formidable clubs in Europe. Bayern's jersey boasts four stars. In order to thank and honour the team's iconic performers of the past, a Bayern Hall of Fame was created, featuring fourteen Germans as well as Brazilian forward Giovane Elber and French defender Bixente Lizarazu.

11
GLOBAL HONOURS
5 UEFA Champions Leagues
1 UEFA Europa League
1 UEFA Cup Winners' Cup
1 UEFA Super Cup
3 FIFA Club World Cups

61
NATIONAL HONOURS
29 German Leagues
19 German Cups
6 German League Cups
7 German Super Cups

2013
German League–
winning jersey

1932
German League–
winning jersey

1967
Cup Winners' Cup–
winning jersey

1974-1976
Two-time Champions
League–winning
jersey

2001
Champions League–
winning jersey

Lizarazu's 69

At the 1954 World Cup finals, FIFA required shirt numbers to be allocated to every squad member. Up until then the highest number a shirt would have was 11. When substitutions were introduced to the game in 1965, higher numbers were commonly seen but rarely at the start of a match. Today, of course, that has all changed. The final jersey that French international Bixente Lizarazu wore in his career, from January 2005 to June 2006, is a striking example: the number he chose was none other than 69. "Such an unlikely number, that got a lot of people talking and smiling," recalls Lizarazu. "We've all got our different superstitions—my lucky number is 3. I still sign autographs by adding a little 3. But when I left Bayern for Marseille in 2004, Lucio, the Brazilian centre-back, took it. When I returned to Munich, I was left looking a bit silly, without a number. I started thinking about other numbers; I was looking for something that people would notice and that was fun. And there it was: 69. It's the year I was born, my height and my weight. At least, it was my weight when I started, because at the time I'd already ballooned to 74 kg," he says, laughing. He adds: "No-one had ever dared to do it before in Germany. In marketing terms, it was a masterstroke. But for me, the erotic connotation was not the first meaning that sprang to mind."

The same could not be said of Dino Drpić. Keen to boost sales of his jersey, the Croatian international defender opted for 69 upon his arrival in Karlsruhe in February 2009. But the German League rejected the idea on the pretext that the digits were too difficult to read from far away. Drpić was forced to wear 11 instead. But that was only part of the story. The Balkan defender had chosen the risqué number on the advice of his wife, Nives Celsius, a former Playboy model who previously confessed publicly that she and Drpić had sex on a football pitch in Croatia. By forbidding the 69—on jerseys at least—the German football authorities were likely trying their best to avoid a future scandal. In August 2010, they prohibited the use of any number over forty.

MUNICH (GERMANY), ALLIANZ ARENA
MAY 13, 2006
Frenchman Bixente Lizarazu celebrates his sixth German League title with Bayern Munich.

Ajax

The Greek origins of Total Football

AJAX'S WHITE JERSEY WITH A BROAD RED STRIPE CONJURES UP MEMORIES—EVEN TODAY—OF SOME OF THE MOST ATTRACTIVE FOOTBALL EVER PLAYED.

Ajax's fabulous history began in 1893, when a group of friends established Union, which would become FC Ajax one year later. But the club's official formation date is March 18, 1900, the day they joined the Amsterdam Football Association and established their home pitch in the east of the city, in the Jewish quarter. Since then, their more fanatical supporters call themselves the *Joden* ("Jews" in Dutch), although the club's roots can actually be traced back to Greek mythology rather than Judaism. A Trojan War-hero, Ajax was known for his derring-do and bravery. His image has appeared on the club crest since September of 1928. So as to distinguish themselves from rivals PSV Eindhoven and Feyenoord, Ajax changed the colour of their jersey several times, having started out in black with a red sash around the waist. This was replaced by red-and-white stripes the day after their first league triumph in 1911. They subsequently opted for a white shirt with a wide, vertical red stripe in the middle of the jersey. It was this jersey that would later become the symbol of the "Total Football" approach, preferred first by Rinus Michels and then Stefan Kovács.

11
GLOBAL HONOURS
4 UEFA Champions Leagues
1 UEFA Europa League
1 UEFA Cup Winners' Cup
3 UEFA Super Cups
2 Intercontinental Cups

62
NATIONAL HONOURS
34 Dutch Leagues
19 Dutch Cups
9 Dutch Super Cups

1992
Europa League–winning jersey

1911
Jersey worn on club's promotion to first division

1971
Champions League–winning jersey

1995
Champions League–winning jersey

2010
Dutch League–winning jersey

Cruyff, from 9 to 14

One of the greatest players of all time, Johan Cruyff did not distinguish himself exclusively with his talent. He also stood out because of the number on the back of his jersey. Starting off with number 9, the "Prince of Amsterdam," his nickname in the city where his mother worked as a cleaner, became known from 1970 onwards for wearing 14, a number traditionally associated with the substitutes' bench. The reason for this unusual choice? While he was injured, his number 9 Netherlands shirt was passed on to Gerrie Mühren. Fully recovered, and possibly a little angry at this turn of events, Cruyff did not ask to have the 9 returned to him, deciding to wear the 14 instead. But the tale did not end there. Famous for smoking cigarettes at halftime, he also distinguished himself from other players by slightly altering his kits. The Netherlands national side at the time wore Adidas shorts and an Adidas jersey with three black stripes down the sleeves. But not Cruyff. Having signed a separate sponsorship deal with Puma, the "Flying Dutchman" refused to wear a jersey manufactured by another brand, and played with just two stripes. This was not an issue during the 1978 World Cup as, unfortunately, Cruyff did not take part. Victim of a kidnapping attempt at his Barcelona residence in 1977, he decided against accompanying his teammates to Argentina, then run by a military dictatorship. The first player to win three European Footballer of the Year awards (1971, 1973, and 1974), Cruyff had nevertheless already earned his stripes in a remarkable career.

AMSTERDAM (THE NETHERLANDS), AMSTERDAM ARENA
NOVEMBER 7, 1978
Johan Cruyff wearing a special jersey during his farewell match with Ajax.

JOHAN CRUYFF

FAREWELL
7-11-78

Atlético River Plate

Los Millonarios back from the brink

IN 2011, THE UNTHINKABLE HAPPENED TO CLUB ATLÉTICO RIVER PLATE. THE OUTFIT, FOUNDED ON MAY 25, 1901, AND THAT DRAWS ITS SUPPORT FROM TRADITIONALLY MIDDLE-CLASS AREAS OF BUENOS AIRES, WAS RELEGATED FOR THE FIRST TIME IN ITS IMPRESSIVE HISTORY.

La Màquina (The Locomotive), a nickname given to River Plate in the 1940s when the team was running away with the Argentinian League, derailed badly on June 26, 2011. For the first time since May 2, 1909, the date of its top-flight debut, River Plate was demoted following an aggregate playoff defeat at the hands of Belgrano (0–2, 1–1). The return leg did not even last the full ninety minutes, as the club's fans invaded the Estadio Monumental pitch towards the end. Aside from the significant damage caused to the stadium, eighty-nine people were injured and another fifty or so were arrested. Once tensions subsided, River Plate fans eventually proved their love for the team's iconic jersey, white with a red diagonal stripe (added by the club's Genoese founders during the Buenos Aires carnival of 1905, for a splash of colour). Supporters turned out in huge numbers to support *Los Millonarios* in the second division, and they had their loyalty rewarded on June 23, 2012, when River returned to the top tier of Argentinian football by beating Almirante Brown 2–0, courtesy of a brace from French striker David Trezeguet.

11

GLOBAL HONOURS

4 Copas Libertadores
1 Copa Sudamericana
3 Recopas Sudamericana
1 Supercopa Libertadores
1 Copa Interamericana
1 FIFA Club World Cup

34

NATIONAL HONOURS

34 Argentinian Leagues

1986
Copa Liberatores–winning jersey

1901- 1905
First jersey

1908
Jersey worn on club's promotion to first division

1920
First Argentinian League–winning jersey

2012
Away jersey

Atlético River Plate

The chicken and the lion

It sounds like a story borrowed from *Aesop's Fables*. The men who ran River Plate, known as *Los Millonarios*, were fed up with being referred to as *Las Gallinas* (The Chickens), ever since their unexpected 4–2 defeat by Uruguayan giants Peñarol in the final of the 1966 Copa Libertadores. During their next league match, Club Atlético Banfield supporters released a hen wearing a red ribbon onto the pitch, and the derogatory nickname stuck. In 1986, then club president Hugo Santilli (1983–89) decided to address the issue by adding the emblem of a lion drawn by Caloi, a famous Argentinian caricaturist, to the chest of the jersey. He also removed the red stripe from the back of the shirt. This change in particular caused an uproar among River supporters, furious that their jersey now looked the same as everyone else's from behind. Curiously, it was while wearing this new look that River enjoyed the most successful period in their history, claiming a thirteenth Argentinian Championship, a maiden Copa Libertadores, a first and only Intercontinental Cup, and a Copa Interamericana, all in the space of just two years. Taking over from Santilli, Alfredo Davicce, who ran the club from 1989 to 1997, removed the lion and restored the stripe. And River Plate would have to wait ten years before winning another international trophy. The moral of the tale? Better to be lionhearted than a chicken.

BUENOS AIRES (ARGENTINA), ESTADIO MONUMENTAL
JUNE 23, 2012
Thanks to a brace from French ace David Trezeguet against Almirante Brown, River Plate make an immediate return to the Argentinian Primera División a year after being relegated for the first time.

Juventus FC

An old lady with an English dress sense

IT WAS THE RESULT OF A MISTAKE IN ENGLAND THAT *LA VECCHIA SIGNORA* GAVE UP HER PINK SHIRTS IN FAVOUR OF THE ICONIC STRIPES.

On November 1, 1897, thirteen young students met on a bench in Turin to establish a multisport club. Aged from fourteen to seventeen, they called it "Sport Club Juventus" ("youth" in Latin). As football strips were not yet readily available, they started off playing in pink, with a tie (or bow tie) and black golf trousers. But as the shirts were of poor quality, they faded quickly. In 1903, they asked Nottingham Forest to deliver some of their red jerseys, but due to a mix-up, black-and-white striped Notts County FC tops were sent to Italy instead, and Juventus have played in *bianconeri* colours ever since, considering them to be "aggressive and powerful." Juventus became powerful indeed on July 24, 1923, the day Edoardo Agnelli, son of Giovanni, founder of Fiat, purchased the club. Since then, the alliance between the Piedmont upper classes and the southern Italian workers in the Turin-based Fiat factories—who support the team—have enabled the club, renamed Juventus Football Club in 1945, to become *La Fidanzata d'Italia* (The Girlfriend of Italy). Yet Juventus' special relationship with England has not been forgotten. In 2011, to inaugurate their new stadium, Juventus invited none other than Notts County FC, placed in the third tier of English football, for a friendly match to mark the occasion, an elegant gesture of gratitude for them giving their stripes.

JUVENTUS

10
GLOBAL HONOURS
2 UEFA Champions Leagues
3 UEFA Europa Leagues
1 UEFA Cup Winners' Cup
2 UEFA Super Cups
2 Intercontinental Cups

56
NATIONAL HONOURS
35 Italian Leagues
13 Italian Cups
8 Italian Super Cups

2015
Champions League–runners-up jersey

1898
First jersey

1930-35
"Quinquennio d'oro" jersey with 5 Scudetti in a row

1984
Italian League and Cup Winners' Cup–winning jersey

1996
Champions League–winning jersey

Juventus FC

Platini gave all he had

On May 17, 1987, after bidding farewell to thirty thousand fans amassed in the dilapidated Stadio Comunale, Michel Platini headed off into the horizon following an exciting Juventus–Brescia clash (3–2), with good memories but without any of the jerseys he wore throughout his immense career. "I don't even have my last Juventus one," explains the former number 10, voted UEFA's president on January 26, 2007. "I really don't have any left at all, in fact. I've given them all away, to friends, to charitable organisations so that they can bring in some money, and to the many, many people who used to ask me when I was younger."

Platini did hold on to some objects, though. "In fact, I only held on to souvenirs that were round, like two of my three European Footballer of the Year [1983, 1984, and 1985] Ballon d'Or trophies. There's one at Mr. Agnelli's house [Giovanni Agnelli, club president while Platini was at Juventus, who passed away on January 24, 2003]. The other two are at home; one's for my son, and the other's for my daughter. Mr. Agnelli asked me one day: 'Is it really made out of gold?' I replied, 'Are you mad? I'd never have given it to you if it was! It's just a golden colour.' In return, he gave me a platinum one. The only thing that I kept that wasn't round is the Olympic torch from the Albertville winter games that I carried in 1992. I still have that in my possession."

Michel Platini wore the iconic jersey of Juventus from 1982 to 1987. His coach Giovanni Trapattoni said of the Frenchman: "He's a genius, a man born to play football."

Inter Milan

International outlook

FOUNDED BY DISSENTING VOICES FROM AC MILAN WHO DISAGREED WITH THE CLUB'S REFUSAL TO FIELD FOREIGNERS, INTERNAZIONALE SUFFERED BETWEEN THE WARS UNDER ITALY'S FASCIST REGIME.

Established on March 9, 1908, at the Orologio restaurant by former members of AC Milan, Internazionale got its name from the desire of its founders to allow foreign players to join the newly formed team. Milan's refusal to let the forty-four Italian and Swiss dissidents play was the principal reason behind their decision to leave the club in order to start up their own. Inter Milan lost their original colours of black and blue in 1928, when the fascist regime, which had prohibited towns from having more than one club, forced them to merge with US Milanese to create an entity known as Ambrosiana, after St. Ambrose, the patron saint of Milan. After a seventeen-year period during which they wore a white jersey with a red cross (the city emblem), they reverted to their original name and colours in 1945. The white shirt would get one more airing, however, as it was used during the 2007–08 season to celebrate Internazionale's centenary. In 1967, they added a star above the club badge, honouring their ten Italian League titles. In May 2011, the iconic jersey became the first football shirt to go into space, when astronaut Paolo Nespoli took it with him on a mission. From international to interplanetary ...

9

GLOBAL HONOURS
3 UEFA Champions Leagues
3 UEFA Europa Leagues
3 Intercontinental Cups

30

NATIONAL HONOURS
18 Italian Leagues
7 Italian Cups
5 Italian Super Cups

2010
Champions League–, Italian Cup–, and Italian League– winning jersey

1910
Italian League– winning jersey

1928-45
The Ambrosiana jersey–white with a red cross

1965
Champions League– winning jersey

1998
Europa League– winning jersey

Facchetti, 3 for eternity

Left-back of the renowned Grande Inter team (1960–68) before going on to become club president in 2004, Giacinto Facchetti made a significant impact on the history of the club he loved, and was the first *nerazzurro* player to have his jersey number (3) retired after his death on September 4, 2006 (aged sixty-four). Argentinian defender Nicolás Burdisso, who wore 3 for Inter at the time of Facchetti's passing, was given the number 16 instead.

The honour, which has been bestowed upon fewer than 150 players worldwide, can also be granted to the living. AC Milan withdrew the number 6 as a tribute to captain Franco Baresi at the end of his career, as well as the 3 worn by Paolo Maldini. In the future, only Christian and Daniele, the former defender's two sons, will have the right to wear the number 3. At Inter, the number 4, worn by the Argentinian international Javier Zanetti, who played 860 matches for Inter between 1995 and 2014, was also retired. Napoli and Brescia retired the number 10 jersey in honour of Diego Maradona and Roberto Baggio respectively. The 14 has not been allocated at Ajax since April 25, 2007, the date of Johan Cruyff's sixtieth birthday.

The practice of retiring fabled jerseys originates from American sport. One of the most famous examples remains the number 23 worn by Chicago Bulls basketball superstar Michael Jordan. In line with a Japanese tradition, supporters can also be paid homage in this manner, and numerous clubs have assigned their loyal fans a perpetual number, often the twelve.

Giacinto Facchetti in 1971.

Santos FC

The Santos spotlight

FROM PELÉ TO NEYMAR, SANTOS HAS PROVIDED A PLATFORM FOR A HOST OF ICONIC PERFORMERS THROUGH THE YEARS. THIS REPUTATION EARNED THE CLUB A FIFTH-PLACED RANKING IN THE FIFA CLUB OF THE CENTURY VOTING IN DECEMBER 2000.

When three men met above a bakery on April 14, 1912, with the intention of forming another football club in São Paulo state, they had no way of knowing they were making history. Santos Futebol Clube, created on that fateful day, would go on to produce and nurture such magicians of the beautiful game as Pelé, Robinho, and Neymar.

One of the founders' first tasks was to select a colour for their new club's jersey. His first choice was a shirt with white, blue, and gold stripes. But as it proved too complicated to make at the time, Santos opted on March 31, 1913 for black-and-white stripes, like the ones used at Juventus. Over time, though, they settled on an all-white strip. A third, turquoise jersey was also worn in 2012 to mark the club's centenary. The town of Santos is located near the city of São Paulo, Brazil's economic heart, and boasts the country's largest seaport. For this reason, the club's founders decided to adopt a sea creature, a whale, as its mascot. Although it does not appear on the club crest, Pelé's former employers have long been nicknamed the *Peixe* (Fish).

8

GLOBAL HONOURS

3 Copas Libertadores
1 Copa CONMEBOL
1 Supercopa Libertadores
1 Recopa Sudamericana
2 Intercontinental Cups

36

NATIONAL HONOURS

8 Brazilian Leagues
22 Campeonatos Paulista
1 Brazilian Cup
5 Torneios Rio – São Paulo

2011
Copa Libertadores–
winning jersey

1912
First jersey

1935
First Campeonato
Paulista–winning
jersey

1963
Copa Libertadores–
winning jersey

2012
Away jersey

Phantom heirs

In 2019, there were already nine of them. A Venezuelan (Yeferson Soteldo), an Argentinian (Walter Montillo), and some Brazilians for the most part (Diego Ribas da Cunha, PH Ganso, Zé Roberto), but apart from the Brazilians, nobody knew them. Yet all had had the immense privilege of wearing the legendary number 10 of King Pelé at Santos FC. Not even Neymar, who was trained at "the Fish," ever wore it. During Neymar's four years there (2009-13), he made do with the 11, in homage to Romário de Souza Faria. This was not because of the promise made by the owners to definitively retire the number 10 after eighteen years of good and loyal service on the part of Pelé (1956–74), who had left to take up one last lucrative gig at New York Cosmos, from June 11, 1975 to August 27, 1977. Indeed, the American club, which vanished in 1985 and reappeared in 2013, never gave the number 10 to anyone else. This was the opposite of what Santos did when, nearly thirty years later, they went back on their pledge, allowing Diego to swap his number 25 for the 10 at the start of the 2003–04 season. If the precise motivations for this about-face, which was an affront to King Pelé, remain vague, in Santos' defense, they were not the only club to have reneged on a promise. In France, Marseille took just a year and a half to recycle Mathieu Valbuena's number 28. It went to Antoine Rabillard, a beginner no less. And when the Cameroonian player Marc-Vivien Foé suffered a heart attack at the age of twenty-eight in the middle of a FIFA Confederations Cup match, on June 26, 2003, in Lyon's Gerland stadium, Lyon initially withdrew his number 17, only to reattribute it five years later (albeit to a fellow Cameroonian player), unlike Manchester City and RC Lens, two of the four clubs for which Foé had played. In Germany, FC Köln reallocated Lukas Podolski's number 10 to Patrick Helmes in 2014, two years after having announced that they were retiring it.

Neymar never dared to wear King Pelé's number 10 at Santos. He made do with Romário's 11.

Manchester United FC

The red devils, still in heaven

ALTHOUGH THEIR GAME HAS BEEN SOMEWHAT IN DECLINE SINCE THEIR MANAGER, SIR ALEX FERGUSON, RETIRED IN 2013, MANCHESTER UNITED CONTINUE TO BE A FLOURISHING CONCERN.

Newton Heath LYR FC, which was founded in 1878 by the employees of a regional railroad company, changed its green-and-gold colours to a red shirt and white shorts in 1902, when it became Manchester United FC. Having learned that the neighbouring rugby league club, Salford, had been nicknamed the Red Devils during a tour to France in the 1930s, Manchester United's manager, Sir Matt Busby, decided to bestow this intimidating moniker on his Busby Babes.

Since the early 1970s, a red devil armed with a trident has been the centre of the coat of arms of a club that seems to have fallen back into line, results-wise, after having taken thirteen of its total twenty Premier League titles and two of its total three UEFA Champions League titles between 1993 and 2013. The club has been controlled by an American family, the Glazers, since May 12, 2005, and remains very profitable, with a record turnover of €711.50 million in the fiscal year 2018–19, a more than 6.5% increase in turnover on the previous year. The main reason for this was the increase in revenue from television rights (+18.1% to €273.50 M) as a result of the new UEFA Champions League broadcasting rights agreement.

8

GLOBAL HONOURS

3 UEFA Champions Leagues
1 UEFA Cup Winners' Cup
1 UEFA Super Cup
1 Intercontinental Cup
2 FIFA Club World Cups

58

NATIONAL HONOURS

20 English Leagues
12 FA Cups
5 English League Cups
21 Charity/Community
   Shields

2008
Champions League–
winning jersey

1902
First red jersey

1968
Champions League–
winning jersey

1999
Champions League–
winning jersey

2013
English League–
winning jersey

MARADONA GOOD PELĒ BETTER GEORGE BEST

Beckham cannot kick with his left foot, can't head the ball, can't tackle and he doesn't score enough goals. Otherwise he's all right.

If I had been born ugly, you would have never heard of Pelé.

In 1969, I gave up women and alcohol. It was the worst 20 minutes of my life.

" I SPENT A LOT OF MONEY ON BOOZE, BIRDS AND FAST CARS. THE REST I JUST SQUANDERED. "

The legend of number 7

It all started in 1961, when Manchester United scout Bob Bishop unearthed a talented fifteen-year-old by the name of George Best. It took just one training session for the club to sign him. Seven years and six trophies later, Best was named European Footballer of the Year for 1968, and the legend of number 7 was born. The phenomenon went far beyond the scope of football. Capable of absolutely anything on, as well as off, the pitch, the gifted winger was the first true rock star footballer of his era. Ousted by United in 1974, he lapsed into alcoholism, suffered financial ruin and died on November 25, 2005, at the age of fifty-nine. A one-time idol of Maradona, Best was given a grand, near-state funeral in Belfast. Bryan Robson wore the 7 jersey from 1981–94, before Eric Cantona, the enfant terrible exiled from France, revived the legend. Following the sudden retirement of "the "King," who was voted best United player of all time by the fans, David Beckham inherited the number. Beckham would in turn hand it down to Cristiano Ronaldo in 2003. When the Portuguese striker joined Real Madrid in 2009, Michael Owen, the 2001 European Footballer of the Year, donned the jersey, but enjoyed less success. Just like the Argentinian Angel Di Maria, the Dutchman Memphis Depay, and the Chilean Alexis Sanchez. The refusal of Japanese international Shinji Kagawa to wear it in 2012 led to Ecuadorian winger Antonio Valencia taking up the mantle. Manchester United fans, however, would love to see a new George Best restore the brilliance of the legendary number 7.

Eric Cantona, affectionately known by Manchester United fans as "King Eric."

Starry mattress makers

MADRID'S SECOND CLUB TOOK THE COLOURS USED IN MATTRESS MAKING, AS WELL AS THE CITY'S SYMBOLS (NOTABLY THE CONSTELLATION URSA MAJOR), TO FORGE ITS IDENTITY.

The club was founded on April 26, 1903, by three Basque students living in Madrid, in homage to the Athletic Bilbao from their childhoods. The original uniform was borrowed from the same blue-and-white stripes of Blackburn Rovers FC's jersey, but on a trip to England in 1911, one of the members of the board was unable to find any spare Rovers kit and brought back some Southampton shirts instead. Luckily, red-and-white-striped material was already commonly used in Spanish mattresses (*colchónes*)—and had the added bonus of costing less to produce—hence the club's nicknames of *Los Colchoneros* (the Mattress Makers) and *Los Rojiblancos* (the Red and White). Missing from the team's original coat of arms were the bear and the strawberry tree—symbols of Madrid—which were added in 1917. Similarly, the seven white stars evoked both the constellation Ursa Major and the flag of the autonomous community of Madrid. Despite this strong local identity, Atlético remained in the shadow of Real Madrid for a long time until the return of its Argentinian former midfielder Diego Simeone in 2011 as its manager. The club is also known as *Los Indios* (the Indians), a moniker that may derive from the traditionally strong South American contingent among Atlético's mainly working-class fans, or else the fact that in colonial times, the Indians were the enemies of *Los Blancos* (the Whites)— nickname of Atlético's rivals, Real Madrid FC.

8

GLOBAL HONOURS

1 UEFA Cup Winners' Cup
3 UEFA Europa Leagues
3 UEFA Super Cups
1 FIFA Club World Cup

22

NATIONAL HONOURS

10 Spanish Leagues
10 Spanish Cups
2 Spanish Super Cups

2014
Spanish League–
winning jersey and
Champions League–
runners-up jersey

1903
First jersey

1966
Spanish League–
winning jersey

2018
UEFA Europa League–
winner jersey

2019
Last jersey worn
by Griezmann

Atlético Madrid

Torres, magic number 9

Atlético's fans didn't resent their club's management giving them the best Christmas gift four days late. On December 29, 2014, seven and a half years after leaving for Liverpool on a £27.8 million transfer, *El Niño* (the Kid), darling of a whole club, finally came home on that blessed day. On January 4, over 45,000 people attended his official presentation at the Vicente Calderón Stadium. Everything was going well for Fernando Torres, in this best of all possible worlds, with one exception: he could not wear his emblematic number 9 again, since it belonged to the Croatian player Mario Mandžukić, who had arrived from Bayern Munich in early summer and had no intention of changing his number midseason. Did this upset El Niño? Let's just say that he scored only six goals in twenty-six matches.

When the Croat international left for Juventus FC at the end of the season, Torres was able to get rid of the 19 he'd inherited when Diego Costa departed for Chelsea, and don number 9 once more. He didn't lose time in sharing his joy on social media, which earned him the following comment from Antoine Griezmann on Twitter: "You're not going to leave it for me? Hahahaha." To which Torres replied: "You're number 7 my friend, which looks very good on you." The return of his favourite number seemed to work wonders, with Torres scoring thirty-two goals (plus fourteen decisive passes) in his last three seasons at Atlético. The double European champion (2008 and 2012) and world champion (2010) then made sure that the number 9 would be his when he moved to the Japanese club Sagan Tosu, where he finished his career on August 23, 2019, at the age of thirty-five.

**MADRID (SPAIN),
WANDA METROPOLITANO**
MAY 20, 2018
El Niño bids farewell to the Madrid fans, wearing the captain's armband and after scoring twice against Sociedad Deportiva Eibar (2–2).

FC Porto

The dragon, a living myth

PORTUGAL'S BIGGEST CLUB USES THE LEGENDARY DRAGON, WHICH GIVES ITS NAME TO THEIR STADIUM, TO STRIKE FEAR IN THE HEART OF OPPONENTS.

Founded on September 28, 1893, Futebol Clube do Porto rose to true prominence in 1904 to become Portugal's most successful club. The blue-and-white colours stem from the desire of those in charge in the early days to bestow their multisport club with a strong national identity. To achieve that, they borrowed the colours from the Portuguese royal flag. Originally, the crest was comprised of a blue ball bearing the initials of the name of the club (FCP), to which the coat of arms of the city of Porto was added in 1922 to symbolise the strong bond between club and city. Above sits a dragon on the city walls, defending it from potential invaders. The dragon mythology relays the idea that the inhabitants of Porto never give up and remain motivated by a spirit of conquest. This symbolism is so far-reaching that when the club's new stadium opened on November 16, 2003, it was christened Estádio do Dragão (Dragon Stadium). *A Chama do Dragão* (flame of the dragon) has ever since enabled FC Porto to shine brightly in the domestic league, as well as in Europe.

7

GLOBAL HONOURS

2 UEFA Champions Leagues
2 UEFA Europa Leagues
1 UEFA Super Cup
2 Intercontinental Cups

69

NATIONAL HONOURS

28 Portuguese Leagues
20 Portuguese Cups
21 Portuguese Super Cups

2004
Champions League–
winning jersey

1935
First Portuguese
League–winning
jersey

1987
Champions League–
and UEFA Super Cup–
winning jersey

2002
Home jersey

2011
Portuguese League–
and Europa League–
winning jersey

FC Porto

The unworn jersey?

It is often possible for a player to pose with his new FC Porto jersey and never, or hardly ever, put it on. This is because, contrary to other countries, Portuguese legislation places no restriction on the number of player loans allowed. And just like Benfica, Porto do not hesitate to use their €100 million budget (the largest in the country) to secure as many players as possible. In 2005, Porto had no fewer than eighty-three players on their books. Since then, that figure has dropped to around sixty. This downsizing has enabled the Dragões to make up for insubstantial domestic TV rights and to help them compete on the European stage. Masters in the art of speculating on young players, especially those from Latin America, with the aim of selling them on for a significant profit, Porto have developed close ties with influential agents by offering them a percentage of resale prices. In Porto, agents have the ideal shop window in which to showcase their players upon their arrival in Europe. This approach has seen the club sell over twenty players for €10 million or more over the last few seasons. Their most jaw-dropping pieces of business involved Brazilian forward Hulk (pictured), who was sold to Zenit St Petersburg for €60 million on September 3, 2012, and Colombian striker Falcao, transferred to Atletico Madrid for €47 million on August 18, 2011, after being bought for €5.5 million from River Plate two years earlier. But of course, those particular stars actually put on the Porto jersey.

Colombian forward Falcao hops on the back of Brazilian strike-partner Hulk. In addition to their many goals, the dynamic duo earned Porto the handsome sum of €107 million when they were sold in 2011 and 2012, respectively.

How the pensioners became champions

LONG VIEWED AS ALSO-RANS IN THE ENGLISH GAME, CHELSEA HAVE BECOME ONE OF THE MOST POWERFUL CLUBS IN THE WORLD.

When property developers renovated Stamford Bridge in 1904, they had planned for every eventuality, except local team Fulham's refusal to play there. Forced to conjure up a resident club, they bestowed the name of the adjacent borough on it, and so Chelsea FC was born on March 10, 1905. Bluish-green jerseys, taken from the colours of the stable belonging to then chairman the Earl of Cadogan, were chosen. The colours became royal blue in 1912. The club emblem, meanwhile, was modified no fewer than seven times. Originally, a Chelsea Pensioner (the term for former members of the British army housed in a nearby nursing home, the Royal Hospital Chelsea) was depicted on the crest. But the image was removed in 1952, when the Pensioners became known as the Blues. A year later, drawing inspiration from the coat of arms of the Metropolitan Borough of Chelsea, Cadogan's own coat of arms, and that of the former Lords of the Manor of Chelsea, a backwards-facing blue lion holding a staff was added to the jersey. A more realistic lion was used between 1986 and 2005, the club's centenary year. Following the takeover by Russian billionaire Roman Abramovich on July 2, 2003, the crest reverted to the traditional lion, a symbol of the past and of a rosy-looking future.

6
GLOBAL HONOURS
1 UEFA Champions League
2 UEFA Europa Leagues
2 UEFA Cup Winners' Cups
1 UEFA Super Cup

23
NATIONAL HONOURS
6 English Leagues
8 FA Cups
5 English League Cups
4 Charity/Community Shields

2012
Champions League–
winning jersey

1905
First jersey

1955
First English League–
winning jersey

1971
First European trophy–
winning jersey
(the Cup Winners' Cup)

1998
Cup Winners' Cup–
winning jersey

Drogba, a fan of the blues

A massive portrait of Didier Drogba looks down on the Shed End, the historic wall that supports the south side of Stamford Bridge. It shows him kissing the Chelsea badge on the Allianz Arena pitch, the stage for the Blues' greatest achievement: their capture of the Champions League. It was Drogba who almost single-handedly delivered the mythical trophy to the Chelsea fans on May 19, 2012, equalising with a header in the 88th minute, then putting away his team's last penalty kick in the ensuing shootout against Bayern Munich (1–1, 4–3 on penalties). The image guarantees the Ivorian's eternal presence in the hearts of the London club's supporters. On November 2, 2012, they even voted him the greatest Chelsea player of all time, ahead of living legends such as Frank Lampard, Gianfranco Zola, and John Terry. And yet the relationship between Drogba and Chelsea's fanbase got off to a rocky start in 2004, as the latter held the former's initial reluctance about joining the club against him for a long period. This would explain why his number 15 jersey (until the departure of Damien Duff in 2006), and then his 11 (picked up by Brazilian midfielder Oscar in 2012), sold in fewer numbers than those of Lampard or Terry, despite the African striker's habit of buying hundreds of them at the club shop to send back to Abidjan. He was not a collector, though. "I've only got three jerseys framed at home: Zidane's, Ronaldo's and Ronaldinho's," he once said. Drogba would have very much liked to add Messi's to his wall before leaving European football, but after having promised him his shirt before the semifinal of the 2012 Champions League, (2–2, April 24; first leg: 1–0), the Argentinian made a sharp exit as soon as the final whistle sounded. Drogba was likely consoled by the fact that T-shirts featuring his own image still sell like hotcakes in Chelsea's shop. He no longer needs to buy them up himself.

**MUNICH (GERMANY),
ALLIANZ ARENA**
MAY 19, 2012
Scorer of Chelsea's equaliser and their last penalty kick in the shootout of the final against Bayern, Ivorian striker Didier Drogba clutches the London club's first Champions League trophy.

Corinthians

The crazy gang

CLUB OF THE STARS (GARRINCHA, RIVELINO, SÓCRATES, AND RONALDO, AMONG OTHERS), CORINTHIANS OCCUPY A SPECIAL PLACE IN THE HEART AND HISTORY OF THE BRAZILIAN PEOPLE.

When immigrant workers from southern Europe established the club on September 1, 1910, they decided to name it after the touring team from London that had just won six matches on Brazilian soil. And so Sport Club Corinthians Paulista came into being. The largest multisport club in São Paulo, it is also one of the most popular. Corinthians claim to have thirty-five million fans, including Lula, former president of Brazil (2003–2011) and Formula 1 drivers Rubens Barrichello and Ayrton Senna (who died in 1994). Their mission statement promises that they will be the team "of the people, by the people and for the people." Although their supporters are nicknamed "*O bando de Loucos*" (the crazy gang), their first administrators were rather conservative, choosing a cream-coloured jersey, which would eventually become white over time. It was not until 1954 that the black shirt with thin white stripes made an appearance. As for the crest, although it dates from 1913, it has been touched up since. The current emblem stretches back to 1940, when an anchor and two oars were added to reflect the club's success in nautical sports.

4
GLOBAL HONOURS
1 Copa Libertadores
2 FIFA Club World Cups
1 Recopa Sudamericana

43
NATIONAL HONOURS
6 Brazilian Leagues
28 Campeonatos Paulista
3 Brazilian Cups
1 Brazilian Super Cup
5 Torneios Rio–São Paulo

2012
Copa Libertadores–
winning jersey

1914
First Campeonato
Paulista–winning
jersey

1954
Campeonato Paulista–
winning jersey

1990
Brazilian League–
winning jersey

2000
First Club World Cup–
winning jersey

A very democratic jersey

Putting on a Corinthians jersey at the start of the 1980s was not a trivial matter. It was a political choice. That was the intent of Brazil captain Sócrates, one of the founders of the Corinthians Democracy initiative in November 1981. This ideological movement was launched to challenge the military dictatorship and to offer the players the opportunity to run the club collectively. Gate receipts and TV rights were distributed between all the club's employees, and between the players, under the guise of win bonuses. In return, they made the decisions about player recruitment and new coaches, which occurred when Zé Maria, former Corinthians defender and 1970 World Cup–winner, was offered the manager's post. They also walked onto the pitch before the final of the 1983 São Paulo State Championship to unfurl a banner that read: "Win or lose, but always within a democracy." This self-management, married to an entertaining brand of football, helped the club enjoy great success both on and off the pitch. "We were fighting for freedom, for a change in our country," explained Sócrates, who sadly passed away on December 4, 2011, at the age of fifty-seven. A qualified doctor of medicine with a strong political conscience, and the elder brother of Raï, also a one-time *Seleção* skipper, Sócrates would often appear on the pitch with the inscription "Democracia Corinthiana" on his jersey, or with messages on his back encouraging people to vote in elections. This mini-republic came to a natural end with the emergence of democracy in Brazil in 1985.

Sócrates celebrates a goal during the Clássico Majestoso between Corinthians and São Paulo in 1982 (right). Much more than a gifted footballer, the "Doctor" was also a man of unshakable political convictions often displayed on his shirt (below).

Borussia Dortmund

A working man's jersey

BORUSSIA DORTMUND, SCHALKE 04'S GREAT RUHR RIVALS, CAN TRACE THEIR ROOTS BACK TO THE WORLD OF STEELWORKERS AND MINERS, AND THEIR COLOURS ARE A REMINDER OF THAT HERITAGE.

The group of local steelworkers and miners was so excited to have established the club on December 19, 1909, they forgot to give it a name. Busy clinking overflowing glasses by that point, they decided to call it "Borussia," the name of their favourite beer (*Borussia* also means "Prussian" in Latin). And so the *Ballspielverein* (ball game) Borussia 1909 Dortmund was born. After starting out in blue and white, BVB 09 (as it was renamed in 1945) later adopted yellow and black—yellow for the overalls worn by its workmen supporters, and black as a tribute to its miner fans. These colours proved to be charmed as, prior to becoming the third German club to hoist the Champions League trophy in 1997 (after Bayern Munich and Hamburg), they were the first to secure European silverware on May 5, 1966 (European Cup Winners' Cup, 2–1 aet over Liverpool). They were also the first German outfit to be floated on the stock exchange in 2000. After flirting with financial ruin five years later, *Die Schwarzgelben* (black and yellows) fought back in style to land a German League and Cup double in 2012.

3
GLOBAL HONOURS
1 UEFA Champions League
1 UEFA Cup Winners' Cup
1 Intercontinental Cup

18
NATIONAL HONOURS
8 German Leagues
4 German Cups
6 German Super Cups

2012
Double-winning jersey
(German League and
German Cup)

1909
First jersey

1966
Cup Winners' Cup–
winning jersey

1997
Champions League–
winning jersey

2017
German Cup–
winning jersey

Borussia Dortmund

The yellow wall

Fans, as well as players, bleed for the shirt in the Cathedral, as Dortmund's stadium, renowned for its unique atmosphere, is commonly known in Germany. The country's largest arena, it was renamed the Signal Iduna Park (after the naming rights were sold to an insurance company) in December 2005. Crippled with debts to the tune of €118 million at the time, Borussia were forced to sell 75% of their stadium, renting it back for €17 million per year so that they could continue to play there. Built for the sole World Cup held in West Germany, and opened on April 2, 1974, it originally boasted a capacity of 54,000. Refurbished numerous times, including for the 2006 World Cup, it has a terrace with space for 27,359 standing fans, 24,454 of which are housed in the Südtribüne. It is 328 feet wide, 170 feet deep, and 131 feet high, and constitutes the largest standing terrace in Europe, and is twice the size of the Anfield kop in Liverpool. What the Germans have come to refer to as *Die Gelbe Wand* (the yellow wall) has turned the Westfalenstadion, as it is still known among Borussia fans, into one of the most colourful and fiery stadiums in the world.

During the 2003–04 season, BVB 09 recorded the highest attendance in Europe with an average of 79,647 supporters at each league match. In 2011–12, only Barcelona attracted more people through their gates.

"The yellow wall must have helped us win 20 times during the 2011–2012 season, at home as well as away. For an opponent, coming up against the wall is an unforgettable experience."

Jürgen Klopp, Borussia Dortmund manager (2008 to 2015)

Proud as a rooster

FOUNDED IN 1882, TOTTENHAM DRAWS ON THE NOBILITY AND BRAVERY (AND SPURS) OF THE ROOSTER, WHICH HAS, SINCE 1921, ADORNED ITS CREST.

When the students of All Hallows Church, North London, decided to found a football club in 1882, they realised that a descendant of Henry Percy (a nobleman who had led the rebellion against King Henry IV of England in 1403) lived in the area. Henry Percy was dubbed Harry Hotspur, owing to his impulsive character, his speed when advancing, and his readiness to attack. He plays a major role in William Shakespeare's play *Henry IV*. In homage, the students named themselves the Spurs and called their club Hotspur FC. In 1884, it became Tottenham Hotspur Football Club (taking the name of its multiethnic neighbourhood), to differentiate itself from another team, which was named London Hotspur).

In 1909, William James Scott, a former player, decided to erect a huge statue of a rooster, with spurs on its ankles, standing atop a ball above the West Stand at White Hart Lane Stadium. This became the club's emblem in 1921, and the rooster now proudly overlooks the Tottenham Hotspur Stadium, which was opened on April 3, 2019. The logo also appears on the club strip—which became white in 1899 in homage to Preston North End FC, the most illustrious team at that time. Hence the Hotspurs' alternate nickname: the Lilywhites.

3
GLOBAL HONOURS
1 UEFA Cup Winners' Cup
2 UEFA Europa Leagues

21
NATIONAL HONOURS
2 English Leagues
8 FA Cups
4 English League Cups
7 Community Shields

2019
Champions League–
runners-up jersey

1951
English League–
winning jersey

1981
FA Cup–
winning jersey

1983
Away jersey for the
centenary of the club

1991
FA Cup–
winning jersey

Harry Kane dreamed of 10

When Harry Kane arrived at Tottenham, aged eleven, he had no ambition to wear the number 9, even though it matched his position on the pitch (striker). No, Kane dreamed of picking up the number 10. "When I was growing up [Robbie] Keane and [Teddy] Sheringham were my idols and they wore 10," he explained to the *Daily Telegraph*. "It's such an iconic number at Spurs, when you look at the players who have worn it— ... [Glenn] Hoddle, [Les] Ferdinand, [Jimmy] Greaves. ... So it was always my dream to wear it." Nevertheless, this extraordinary striker had to be patient. After starting with number 37 on his back, then number 18, he only received 10 at the beginning of the 2015–16 season, following the departure of Togolese player Emmanuel Adebayor. "When I knew 10 was available I just wanted it. I love this club and to be wearing number 10 for Tottenham is amazing for me. I could not resist."

Neither could Kane resist playing with the number 9 when captaining England during the 2018 World Cup, having expressly asked the England team manager, Gareth Southgate (who had just named him captain), for it. As soon as he got it, he passed his number 10 to Raheem Sterling. In Kane's eyes, the number 9 symbolised his new status and his role as striker for the Three Lions. This might seem a surprising choice when one remembers that in the 1986 World Cup, Gary Lineker won the Golden Boot award with the number 10 on his back. Yet the number 9 didn't stop Harry Kane doing as well as Lineker at the 2018 World Cup, in Russia, where he too picked up the Golden Boot with six goals, before returning to his number 10 at Tottenham and continuing to embody his club's motto: *Audere est facere* (To Dare Is to Do).

**MADRID (SPAIN),
WANDA METROPOLITANO**
JUNE 1, 2019
Kane takes on Georgino Wijnaldum in the Champions League final against Liverpool, which Tottenham lost 2-0.

Benfica

The 200,000-member club

FLOATED ON THE STOCK EXCHANGE SINCE MAY 22, 2007 (15 MILLION SHARES), BENFICA, ONE OF LISBON'S TWO GIANT CLUBS ALONGSIDE SPORTING, BOAST A LEVEL OF POPULAR SUPPORT IN PORTUGAL THAT ONLY PORTO COME CLOSE TO.

On February 28, 1904, twenty-four students formed a multisport club at the Franco pharmacy on the Rua de Belém, in the southwest of Lisbon. Naming it "Benfica," after one of the city's civil parishes, they decided the team would wear red and white. Their motto—E Pluribus Unum (Out of many, one)—was inscribed on the crest, which took the shape of a bicycle wheel (cycling being another sport practised at the Benfica club) surrounding a red-and-white shield. The same motto also happens to appear on the Great Seal of the United States. Over a century later, on September 29, 2009, Benfica registered its 200,000th *sócio* (paying member) across the world. In the meantime, after having abandoned their policy of signing only Portuguese players in the 1970s, they placed three stars above the club crest, representing the thirtieth Portuguese League title, attained in 1994. They won their first championship back in 1936, and now have about seventy trophies in their display cabinet.

2
GLOBAL HONOURS
2 UEFA Champions Leagues

78
NATIONAL HONOURS
37 Portuguese Leagues
26 Portuguese Cups
7 Portuguese League Cups
8 Portuguese Super Cups

2010
Portuguese League–
winning jersey

1904
First jersey

1936
First Portuguese
League-winning
jersey

1962
Away jersey

1973
Portuguese League–
winning jersey

Benfica

Where eagles dare

The animal world has often inspired club founders pondering over potential crests. A basic method of communication, the chosen beast— often ravenous, carnivorous, or wild—is meant to embody the values of a club. Benfica settled on an Iberian Eagle, which symbolises authority, independence, and nobility. An eagle named Vitoria (Victory) is actually released over the Estádio da Luz prior to each home fixture and is depicted with its wings wide open on the club crest. Benfica are not alone in using an eagle in this way. Italian outfit Lazio do the same before their matches at Rome's Stadio Olimpico, while Palermo's badge displays the white and gold eagle from the town's coat of arms. In Greece, the bird finds itself in great demand. Emblem of the Ecumenical Patriarchate of Constantinople, it figures on the crests of AEK Athens, PAOK Salonika, and Doxa Drama. In Turkey, Beşiktaş' eagle is black, like the black on the club's jersey. The same goes for Nice in France, for Pirin Blagoevgrad in Bulgaria and for Spartak Nalchik in Russia, but not for their compatriots of Sibir Novosibirsk, who prefer a blue eagle, as do Crystal Palace (England). Eintracht Frankfurt's eagle is red, while in the Ivory Coast (Africa Sports National), Hungary (Ferencváros), and Morocco (Raja Casablanca), the bird is green. Mexican heavyweights Club América boast a golden eagle, and Manchester City's has its tongue sticking out. National teams are also not averse to using the large bird of prey as a symbol. Mali (The Eagles) and Tunisia (The Eagles of Carthage) are just two examples. What all of these jerseys have in common is that their fans are unsympathetic to any attempts to remove the powerful image. When Poland's kit manufacturer replaced their eagle with a less visible variant of the national emblem, fan protests forced them to put it back in its rightful place ahead of Euro 2012, the competition that Poland cohosted with Ukraine.

Águia Vitória, the eagle that soars above the stands prior to each match held at the Estádio da Luz, has appeared on the Benfica crest for over a hundred years.

Arsenal

Victory in white sleeves

FOUNDED ON MAY 1, 1886, THE CLUB WITH THE MOTTO "VICTORIA CONCORDIA CRESCIT" ("VICTORY THROUGH HARMONY") HAS CHANGED ITS NAME AND SHIRT NUMEROUS TIMES.

Arsenal's initial name was Dial Square FC (a reference to a sundial at the factory entrance). The club was later named Royal Arsenal and Woolwich Arsenal. Relegated and on the verge of bankruptcy, the club was bought in 1910, and soon moved to the Arsenal Stadium in Highbury, North London, in 1913, whereupon it was renamed Arsenal FC. As it was the first London club to gain promotion to the first division in 1904, club officials were unable to find appropriate jerseys in the London area. Instead, they appealed to Nottingham Forest, who sent them a supply of dark red jerseys, Forest's colour of choice at the time. Over the years, the dark red was significantly lightened, and in 1933, white sleeves were introduced for a home match against Liverpool. The change helped the team stand out against the all-red Liverpool, and the now famous white sleeves have been featured ever since, except for two seasons between 1965 and 1967 when all-red shirts were preferred, and during the 2005–06 season when Arsenal reverted to their original dark red colours to mark their last campaign at Highbury. Adding white to the sleeves seems to have been a wise decision as throughout the twentieth century, Arsenal were the best team in England with an average league position of 8.5, just ahead of all-red Liverpool.

2

GLOBAL HONOURS

1 UEFA Europa League
1 UEFA Cup Winners' Cup

43

NATIONAL HONOURS

13 English Leagues
13 FA Cups
2 English League Cups
15 Charity/Community Shields

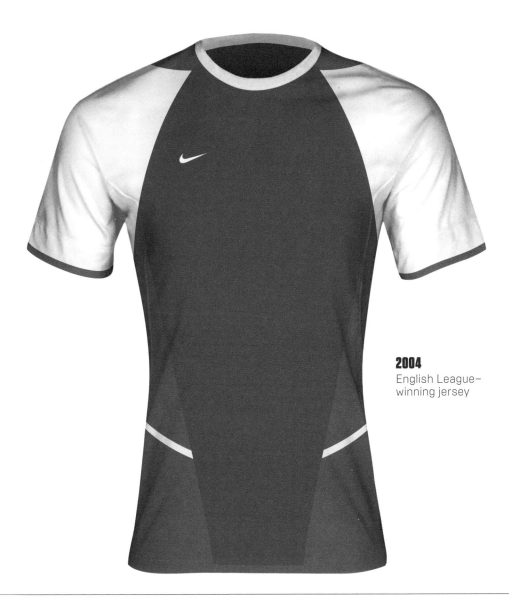

2004
English League–
winning jersey

1906
Home jersey

1933
English League–
winning jersey

1994
Cup Winners' Cup–
winning jersey

2013
Home jersey

Arsenal

Henry, Arsenal's twelfth man

Since December 10, 2011, a statue of Thierry Henry has stood outside the Emirates Stadium. It captures the Frenchman doing his traditional goal celebration.

And suddenly, as if by magic, the statue erected in Thierry Henry's honour on December 10, 2011, on the Emirates Stadium forecourt, came to life. The French forward climbed down from his pedestal to take to the pitch and score once again for Arsenal. The fans' wildest dreams had become reality during an amazing FA Cup evening against Leeds. The turn of events cost British bookmakers, who were not convinced by the comeback, the princely sum of €1.2 million. "Titi is a legend here. He left an unforgettable imprint on the history of the club. His goal only serves to further enhance his reputation," said a delighted Arsène Wenger at the time. When his former protégé (1999–2007) came back to Arsenal to keep himself fit during the MLS off-season, the experienced coach offered him a six-week contract. "It was difficult for me to say no," explained the New York Red Bulls frontman, voted greatest Arsenal player of all time and best foreign player to ever grace the Premier League in 2008. Henry wore the number 14 jersey in his first spell with Arsenal. He chose 12, the number on his back when he lifted the World Cup in 1998 and triumphed at the European Championship in 2000. It was in that number that he hit the back of the net against Blackburn (7–1) and Sunderland (2–1). He brought his short assignment to a close by appearing in a seventh match, a 4–0 Champions League loss in Milan on February 16, 2012. And then the Gunners' all-time leading goalscorer (228 goals) continued on his way. His statue, on the other hand, will remain forever.

With 228 goals to his name, Thierry Henry is the Gunners' all-time top-scorer.

Arsenal Women FC

Star women

Founded in 1987, Arsenal Women FC today holds the most titles of any English women's club, as well as being the first and only English women's team to win the Champions League. Arsenal Women Football Club was founded in 1987 by Vic Akers (the long-term kit manager of Arsenal's men's team). He managed the club for twenty-two years before becoming its honorary president. The ladies took their first major title, the FA Women's National League Cup, in 1992, the year in which they also gained promotion to the FA Women's Premier League. The club turned professional in 2004, and moved to Meadow Park, where they shared the pitches with the boys of Boreham Wood FC, in Hertfordshire, to the north of London. Incidentally, the town of Borehamwood has been nicknamed the "British Hollywood," owing to the several film studios that have been based there over the decades. Among the productions shot there were several of the *Indiana Jones* and *Star Wars* films. The legend that is Arsenal Women (holder of the most titles of any English women's club) was written by stars such as English striker Marieanne Spacey-Cale (1993–2002), English defender Faye White (1996–2013), and the Irish goalie Emma Byrne (2000–16). In 2007, the club became the first British winner of the UEFA Women's Champions League.

Olympique de Marseille

Straight for goal

FOLLOWING THE MOTTO INSCRIBED ON THEIR CLUB CREST TO THE LETTER, MARSEILLE INCREASED THE PROFILE OF THEIR JERSEY BY PLAYING AN EFFECTIVE STYLE THAT TOOK FRANCE AND EUROPE BY STORM.

The details of the foundation of Olympique de Marseille are as murky as a bowl of bouillabaisse, the fish stew that originated in the southern French city. Some believe the club was founded in August 1899, by way of a merger between the fencing club L'Epée and the Football Club de Marseille, who are said to have bequeathed the famous "Droit au but" ("Straight for goal") motto that adorned the badge up until 1935 and then again after 1986. For others, l'OM, officially recognised by law on December 12, 1900, was formed in 1892. The club itself has opted for 1899 as its official founding date. The colour white was adopted right from the start as a nod towards the purity of the Olympian ideal extolled by Pierre de Coubertin—all of the athletes at the first modern Olympic Games, held in Athens in 1896, were dressed in white. Marseille have constantly changed both their away and third colours, ever since the return of Adidas as kit supplier in 1974 (Adidas was replaced by Reebok and Mizuno from 1994 to 1996, and again by Puma since July 1, 2018). Despite marketing concerns, the home top kept its original white. It also boasts a gold star above the crest, which was added in 1993 to mark Marseille's historic Champions League victory. To date, they remain the only French side to have won Europe's premier club tournament.

DROIT AU BUT

1

GLOBAL HONOUR

1 UEFA Champions League

24

NATIONAL HONOURS

9 French Leagues
10 French Cups
3 French League Cups
2 French Super Cups

1993
Champions League–
winning jersey

1924
First French Cup–
winning jersey

1998
Centenary jersey

2004
UEFA Europa League–
runners-up jersey

2010
French League–
winning away jersey

Olympique de Marseille

Papin's benevolent streak

A Bordeaux-based friend of Jean-Pierre Papin broke down in tears the day the French striker gave him a case full of jerseys as a present. "I had about 60 of them, including some old Soviet and Yugoslav ones," recalls the 1991 European Footballer of the Year. "I knew he collected football jerseys, and I preferred to see them framed on his wall rather than get eaten by moths," he continues. Papin demonstrated the same type of generosity throughout his career. "The whole point of a jersey is to provide people with pleasure. Players should hand out ten a day to supporters who don't have enough money to buy one. That's what I did, to the extent that people—who I often don't remember giving anything to—still come up to me today to show me them," says the former France international. The five-time French League top goalscorer (1988–92) did keep one jersey for himself, the one he wore when bidding farewell to Marseille supporters at the Stade Vélodrome on April 25, 1992, a match in which the home side defeated Cannes 2–0. "It's symbolic; in fact, I kept one jersey from six of the clubs I played for, Valenciennes, Bruges, Marseille, Milan, Bayern Munich and Bordeaux. A lack of space means I don't have one from my last club, Guingamp (1998), because I had them transformed into chairs by Laurent Pardo, a French designer. The jerseys were used to upholster the chairs, which I've arranged around the poker table in my house in Arcachon. The only thing I collect is balls. I've got some made of glass, wood, leather and, of course, one made of gold: my Ballon d'Or European Footballer of the Year award. That sits on the living room table, because I want to see it every day!" he concludes with a smile.

Jean-Pierre Papin's acrobatic volleys gave birth to a new French footballing term: Papinade.

A citizen's club

FOUNDED BY A VICAR'S WIFE WITH SOCIAL AIMS, MANCHESTER'S SECOND CLUB CONSIDERS ITSELF TO BE THE CLUB OF THE CITY'S INHABITANTS, HENCE ITS NICKNAME: THE CITIZENS.

Anna Connell, the wife of the vicar of St. Mark's parish, was concerned at seeing the youth of West Gorton spending their money in the pubs. So, in 1880, she decided to encourage them to play sports by starting a cricket club, followed by a football club. The players of St. Mark's FC initially wore black shirts stamped with Maltese crosses, white shorts, and black-and-white–striped socks. The colour blue first appeared in 1887, when the kit was a white shirt with dark blue stripes (later changed to light blue). The club was first called St. Mark's Gorton, and underwent two name changes before going bankrupt and definitively taking the name Manchester City FC on April 16, 1894. The strip changed again to a sky-blue shirt—known as Cambridge blue—with white shorts and dark blue socks. The seventh, and most recent, club badge (introduced in 2016) still features the city's coat of arms, but the golden eagle, a key element of the 1997 badge, was replaced by a ship symbolising the Manchester Ship Canal. The baby blue of the water the ship sails on is crossed by three light blue diagonals that represent Manchester's three rivers, emblazoned with a Lancashire rose.

1
GLOBAL HONOUR
1 UEFA Cup Winners' Cup

24
NATIONAL HONOURS
6 English Leagues
6 FA Cups
6 English League Cups
6 Charity/Community Shields

2019
English League-
winning jersey

1884
First jersey

1937
English League-
winning jersey

1956
FA Cup-
winning jersey

1970
Cup Winners' Cup-
winning jersey

Blue skies, finally

For a long time, the two predominant colours in Manchester—that large, formerly industrial city in northeast England—were the gray pouring from the factory chimneys, and the red of Manchester United (the Red Devils). But ever since Manchester City FC was bought by the Abu Dhabi United Group, in September 2008, life in Manchester has also taken on a sky-blue hue. Al Mubarak's seemingly unlimited financial support has seen the Citizens shine with their luster of old. In 2012, after a drought of forty-four years, the Sky Blues reached the pinnacle of English football for the third time in their history, when they won the Premier League. The following years saw them add three other championship titles, as well as several English cups (FA, League, Community Shield) to their collection.

Throughout this golden period, the Manchester City shirt was stamped with the Nike logo, in a sponsorship deal that ran from 2013 to 2019. But the American giant, which was paying the club £20 million per season, had no hard feelings. Indeed, Nike even decided to celebrate these seven seasons with a collector's shirt. This limited-edition farewell jersey, individually numbered from 1 to 6,000, combined nine graphic elements that were emblematic of the years of their partnership, in which City won six major trophies, notably the 2017–18 Premier League, when City set a record for the number of Premier League points won in a season (one hundred). Nike is used to making such "mash-up" shirts, having already done so to celebrate the twentieth anniversaries of its partnerships with FC Barcelona and Inter Milan. Now it's up to Puma—who have become City's latest kit sponsor, at a cost of £65 million per year—to demonstrate that level of creativity.

**MANCHESTER (ENGLAND),
OLD TRAFFORD**
APRIL 24, 2019
Before kickoff of the Manchester derby, Raheem Sterling shows off the collector's edition of the shirt celebrating the fruitful partnership between Nike and the Citizens.

Logo, you got the look

IN 2013, A DESIRE TO GROW THE PARIS SG BRAND INTERNATIONALLY LED ITS QATARI OWNERS TO GET RID OF ALL SYMBOLS ON THE LOGO THAT MIGHT BE CONSIDERED NEGATIVE. IT WASN'T A REVOLUTION BUT A MODERNISATION.

Keen to make Paris Saint-Germain one of the biggest sports brands in the world, the club's new Qatari owners (since June 30, 2011) decided to get rid of certain symbols on the logo. Unveiled on February 22, 2013, this logo's new look was designed around two key symbols—Paris and the Eiffel Tower—and incorporated a brighter red. Since the relative youth of Paris SG (no longer PSG) was a handicap when compared with other big clubs—which dated their starts from the 1800s—its year of founding (1970) was removed, as was the white cradle symbolising the birth of King Louis XIV in the outer Paris suburb of Saint-Germain-en-Laye. The "Saint-Germain" part (considered confusing) was detached from the word "Paris" and placed at the bottom in smaller lettering. Only the fleur-de-lis—representing royalty and purity—was retained and gilded, although, like the Eiffel Tower, it has sometimes been replaced by the Jumpman logo, ever since Paris SG signed an exclusive three-year partnership (on September 13, 2018) with Jordan Brand, subsidiary of the American sports equipment and clothing company Nike. Paris SG's current slogan, "*Revons plus grand*," ("Dream Bigger") is a riff on Nike's famous "Dream Big."

Logo
from 1970 to 1972

Logo
from 1992 to 1996

Logo
from 2002 to 2013

1

**GLOBAL
HONOUR**

1 UEFA Cup Winners' Cup

37

**NATIONAL
HONOURS**

8 French Leagues
12 French Cups
8 French League Cups
9 French Super Cups

2019
French League–
winning jersey

1975
Away jersey worn
on club's promotion
to first division

1986
French League–
winning jersey

1994
French League–
winning jersey

1996
Cup Winners' Cup–
winning jersey

Paris Saint-Germain

Mbappé, stronger than Neymar

You couldn't make it up. According to a survey commissioned by Kylian Mbappé's entourage from Nielsen (a company specializing in marketing and brand value surveys), Paris SG's incredible striker enjoyed a better image in 2018 than Neymar … in Brazil. This, of course, came on the back of France's world champion title earned in Russia, but it says much about Mbappé's endlessly growing popularity. As for Neymar, the Seleção's number 10 lost ground to the Frenchman, owing to Neymar being considered a more divisive figure in his country, having been penalized for unbecoming behaviour, and disappointing performances on the pitch.

Mbappé's kit supplier, Nike, and Bulk Homme—a Japanese cosmetics brand that became a sponsor both of Mbappé personally and his club—clearly weren't wrong to take Mbappé on a tour of the United States and Japan during the course of summer 2019. Ever since his world championship title, Mbappé has seen his brand soar across not only France, but all over the planet. Indeed, one need look no further than the sales of his official shirts. Mbappé is now the player who moves the most product, be that with Paris SG or the national team—five times more than even Antoine Griezmann, and seven to eight times more than Paul Pogba.

Although Neymar was solely responsible for 300,000 of the 900,000 shirts sold by Paris SG during his first season in the French capital (2017–18), the Frenchman has since caught up the Brazilian. In 2018–19, Mbappé sold more shirts than Neymar. Even when it comes to merchandise, Mbappé is worth his weight in gold.

**PARIS (FRANCE),
PARC DES PRINCES**
OCTOBER 7, 2018
Mbappé hugs Neymar after scoring four goals in thirteen minutes against Lyon in League One (5–0).

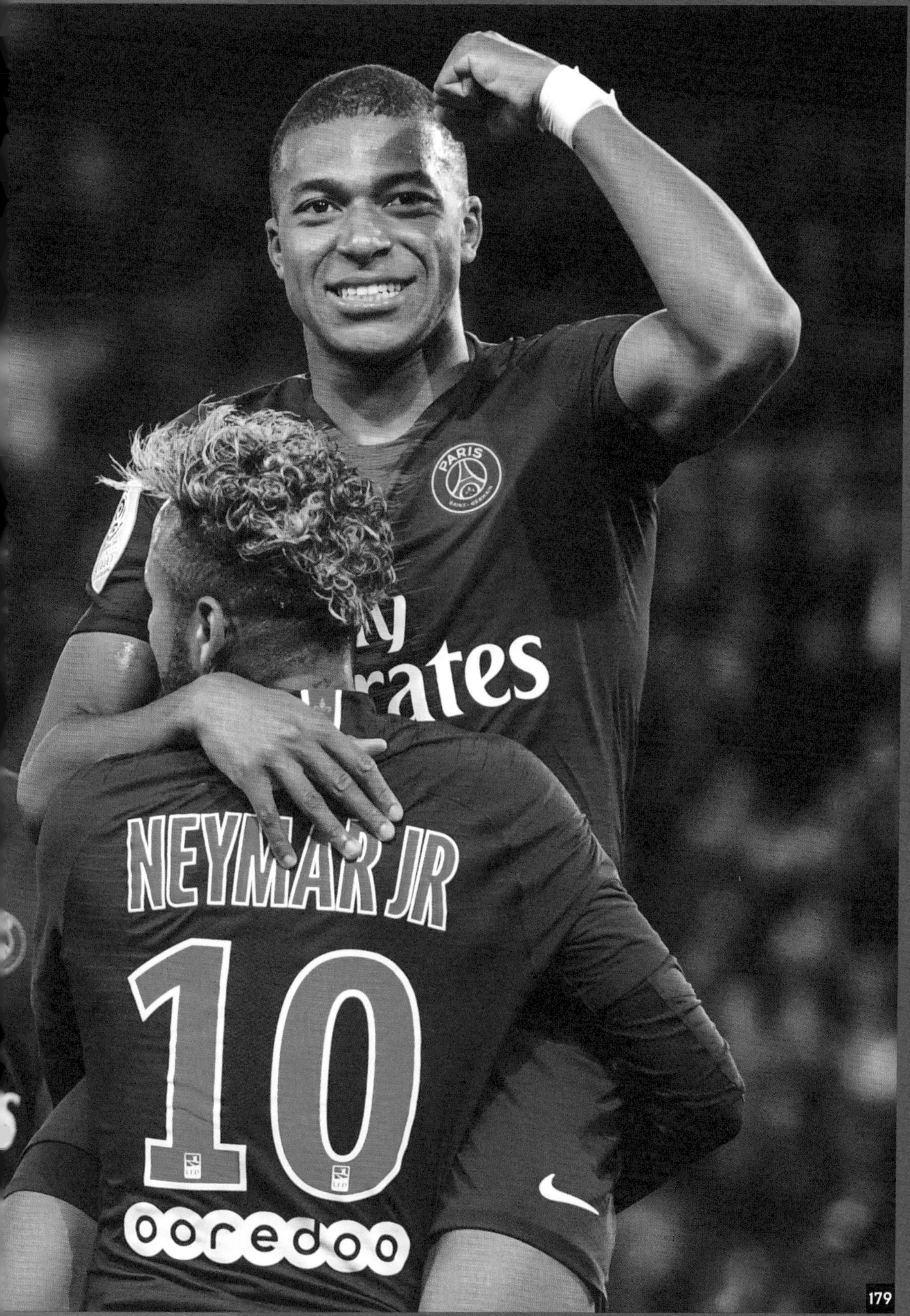

NEYMAR JR
10
ooredoo
rates
PARIS

AS Saint-Étienne

A grocer's smock

SAINT-ÉTIENNE IS THE ONLY FRENCH CLUB WITH A TRICOLOUR STAR—SYMBOLISING ITS TEN CHAMPIONSHIP TITLES—AND IT OWES ITS GREEN COLOUR TO THE FRENCH SUPERMARKET CHAIN CASINO, WHOSE OWNER FOUNDED THE CLUB.

His bust sits proudly beside the entrance to the locker room of the stadium that bears his name, for the Association Sportive de Saint-Étienne owes everything to Geoffroy-Guichard, owner of the Casino supermarket chain, who founded the original club in 1919. Green was the colour of the shutters of his grocery stores, and the club—initially called the Amicale des Employés de la Société des Magasins Casino before adopting its current name in 1927 and turning professional in 1933—has always played with this colour. But it took the spread of colour television in the 1970s—a period when Saint-Étienne was setting European football alight—for the club to become known as *Les Verts* (the Greens). Along with the Reds of Liverpool, Saint-Étienne remains one of the few teams known throughout the world for the colour of its strip. In 1968, the club adopted the black panther as its emblem (following a competition involving the Saint-Étienne art school), in homage to their Malian striker Salif Keïta, who was awarded the first ever Ballon d'Or Africain, in 1970. The panther has now disappeared from the club's badge, but since 1993, it has been surmounted by a tricolour star (blue, white, and red) in honour of AS Saint-Étienne being the only club (at least until 2021) to have won ten French championship titles.

0
GLOBAL HONOUR

17
NATIONAL HONOURS
10 French Leagues
6 French Cups
1 French League Cup

1976
Champions League–
runners-up jersey

1933
First jersey

1957
French League–
winning jersey

1981
French League–
winning jersey

2013
French League Cup–
winning jersey

AS Saint-Étienne

Cheeky Spider-Man

Jérémie Janot had prepared his stunt well. Already wearing a Spider-Man shirt, he waited until the team posed for the official photo of the AS Saint-Étienne versus FC Istres game (2–0) on May 21, 2005, before pulling the Spider-Man mask from his shorts and putting it on, to the general surprise of everyone there. "Then I ran across the pitch and only took it off once I was in my goal. The craziest thing was the way the stadium just exploded that day," said the Saint-Étienne goalkeeper. The image went around the world. But Janot, who considered himself "a fan who kept goal," had previous history as a prankster. With the support of regional sports-wear firm Duarig, Janot had often worn a special handmade shirt for big occasions. "During one derby, I taunted the Brazilians of Lyon by wearing an Argentina shirt," he said. Other outings saw him dressed in military camouflage, a paintball outfit, the Pink Panther, the polka-dotted King of the Mountains jersey from the Tour de France (in homage to Richard Viren-que), and that of the Paris rugby team Stade Français in Marseille (Paris SG's big rival). "But after reaching a peak with Spider-Man, we didn't want to fall into stupid or ridiculous one-upmanship, and end up doing one outfit too many. So that's why we stopped, just before Darth Vader!"

Pierre-Emerick Aubameyang, a fan of Marvel superheroes, picked up the torch by putting on a Spider-Man mask too, in celebration of his goal on October 26, 2012, when Saint-Étienne played Stade Rennes (2-0). At Arsenal, he took out a Black Panther mask (again when playing Rennes) in the quarterfinal return leg of the UEFA Europa League (3-0), on March 14, 2019 (away leg: 1-3). He had already used others during his time at Dortmund

(2013–18), which led him to join CR7 in signing a lifetime contract with Nike (in March 2017), becoming "the Masked Finisher."

At Borussia Dortmund, Pierre-Emerick Aubameyang imitated Jérémie Janot, his former goalie at Saint-Étienne.

Saint-Étienne Saint-Étienne Saint-Étienne
BANQUE
KONICA MINOLTA

Olympique Lyonnais Féminin

Hungry like lionesses

LYON'S WOMEN'S FOOTBALL TEAM (WHICH BECAME PART OF OLYMPIQUE LYONNAIS IN 2004) HAS WON NEARLY ALL THE TITLES SINCE 2007, BOTH IN FRANCE, AND AT A EUROPEAN LEVEL.

Lyon has had a women's football team since 1970—as a part of the FC Lyon sports club—and had taken four French championship titles (1991, 1993, 1995, and 1998), but had to wait until the summer of 2004 to officially become part of Olympique Lyonnais. Three years later Lyon pulled off a record men's-women's double. For the first time in France, the same club was champion of both the men's and the women's first division. Olympique Lyonnais FC went one better in 2008, when the women's side won their first double (French Cup and French championship)—that is to say, exactly the same as the men's side. From that date on, Lyon's women's team was the best in the world, taking all the French championship titles, as well as six UEFA Women's Champions League titles (from eight finals played) between 2011 and 2019. A record.

Today, it is thanks to the women, who wear the same crest and the same shirt as the men (white with red and blue panels—the colours of the city of Lyon), that Olympique Lyonnais performs at the highest level. And knowing the all-devouring ambition of its chairman, Jean-Michel Aulas, this hegemony is far from over.

6
GLOBAL HONOURS
6 UEFA Women's Champions Leagues

22
NATIONAL HONOURS
13 Women's French Leagues
8 Women's French Cups
1 Trophée des Championnes

2019
UEFA Women's
Champions League–
winning jersey

2005
First jersey

2008
Women's French Cup–
winning jersey

2011
UEFA Women's
Champions League–
winning jersey

2012
UEFA Women's
Champions League–
winning jersey

Hegerberg, forever first

The Norwegian international Ada Hegerberg was only twenty-three years old when she walked up the steps to the Grand Palais in Paris (on December 3, 2018) in a gold dress to pick up the first ever women's Ballon d'Or. Six months earlier, Olympique Lyonnais FC, her club since 2014, had already showered her in silver, so to speak, offering her the highest-ever contract in the history of women's football (between €400,000 and €500,000 gross a year) in exchange for extending her contract until June 30, 2021.

Hegerberg's talent is priceless. When she won the Ballon d'Or, this unmatched goal scorer had already notched up an incredible record of 185 goals in 149 matches, played while wearing the Lyon shirt, including an astounding hat trick in sixteen minutes flat during the final of the UEFA Women's Champions League against FC Barcelona Women (4–1, May 18, 2019). She was the first woman to pull off such a feat in a UWCL final, to the great joy of her sister, Andrine—two years her elder—against whom she used to play when Andrine was a midfielder for Paris SG (2018–19). Yes, football is a family affair for the Hegerbergs: their father, Stein Erik, was a midfielder before turning to coaching, while their mother, Gerd, was an international striker. Ada Hegerberg has been in a relationship with Thomas Rogne—another Norwegian international, and a centre-back—since 2016 (they married in May 2019).

LYON (FRANCE), GROUPAMA STADIUM
DECEMBER 5, 2018
Ada Hegerberg shows off her Ballon d'Or at the Lyon's men's team's League One match against Stade Rennes (0–2).

The devourers devoured

FFC FRANKFURT HAS BEEN ONE OF THE BASTIONS OF EUROPEAN WOMEN'S FOOTBALL, ALONG WITH OLYMPIQUE LYONNAIS FC, BUT THEY RECENTLY AGREED TO JOIN EINTRACHT FRANKFURT (A MEN'S TEAM), STARTING WITH THE 2020–21 SEASON.

Women's football was first played in Frankfurt in 1973, but it was not until August 27, 1998, that Frauen-Fußball-Club Frankfurt was born—a female player takes pride of place in the centre of its logo. 1. FFC Frankfurt has fiercely cherished its status as an independent women's football club for many years. Indeed, with twenty titles in two decades, including four UEFA Women's Champions League titles from six finals, it is Germany's most successful women's football club, and Europe's second—behind Olympique Lyonnais Féminin. However, its recent decline ended up convincing its directors of the necessity of joining the men's team. Starting with the 2020–21 season, 1. FFC Frankfurt will be absorbed into Eintracht Frankfurt, a club in the Bundesliga. "We are extremely happy that the Eintracht management decided to forge a joint future," Siegfried Dietrich (the manager of 1. FFC Frankfurt) says happily. "It is now up to us to support our members, our fans and our sponsors on this new path." And to enable Frankfurt to retake its position as the stronghold of European football.

4
GLOBAL HONOURS
4 UEFA Women's Champions Leagues

16
NATIONAL HONOURS
7 Women's German Leagues
9 Women's German Cups

2015
UEFA Women's
Champions League–
winning jersey

1999
Double-winning jersey
(German League
and German Cup)

2001
Women's German
League–
winning jersey

2006
UEFA Women's
Champions League–
winning jersey

2014
Women's German
Cup–winning jersey

Umeå IK

Early pioneers

THIS SWEDISH CLUB PLAYED IN THE FIRST THREE FINALS OF THE UEFA WOMEN'S CHAMPIONS LEAGUE, BUT HAS SINCE LOST ITS LUSTRE, OWING TO SERIOUS ECONOMIC PROBLEMS.

The Umeå IK multisports club (bowling, wrestling, figure skating, etc.) was founded on July 20, 1917, by five boys (who chose a black-and-yellow shirt). But it was not until 1985 that the women's team really took off, when they played in the fourth division. By the 2000s, the club dominated both the Swedish game and the rest of Europe, thanks largely to Malin Moström—also captain of the national side (113 caps)—whose number 6 is the only shirt number to have been retired by the only club for which she ever played (from 1995 to December 2006).

Over the past couple of decades, Umeå IK has focussed mainly on women's football and their youth team. The club played in the first three finals of the UEFA Women's Champions League (2001–04) and won two of them. Driven strongly by the Brazilian star Marta (Vieira da Silva), who was crowned Best FIFA Women's Player six times (2006–10 and 2018), Umeå IK played two more finals (in 2007 and 2008) and lost both. After suffering serious financial problems (2016 saw a new bankruptcy threat), Sweden's second most successful club, after FC Rosengård, is now looking for a fresh start.

2
GLOBAL HONOURS
2 UEFA Women's Champions Leagues

13
NATIONAL HONOURS
7 Women's Swedish Leagues
4 Women's Swedish Cups
2 Svenska Supercupens

2004
UEFA Women's
Champions League–
winning jersey

2007
Women's Swedish
League–
winning jersey

2008
UEFA Women's
Champions League–
runners-up jersey

2012
Home jersey

2015
Home jersey

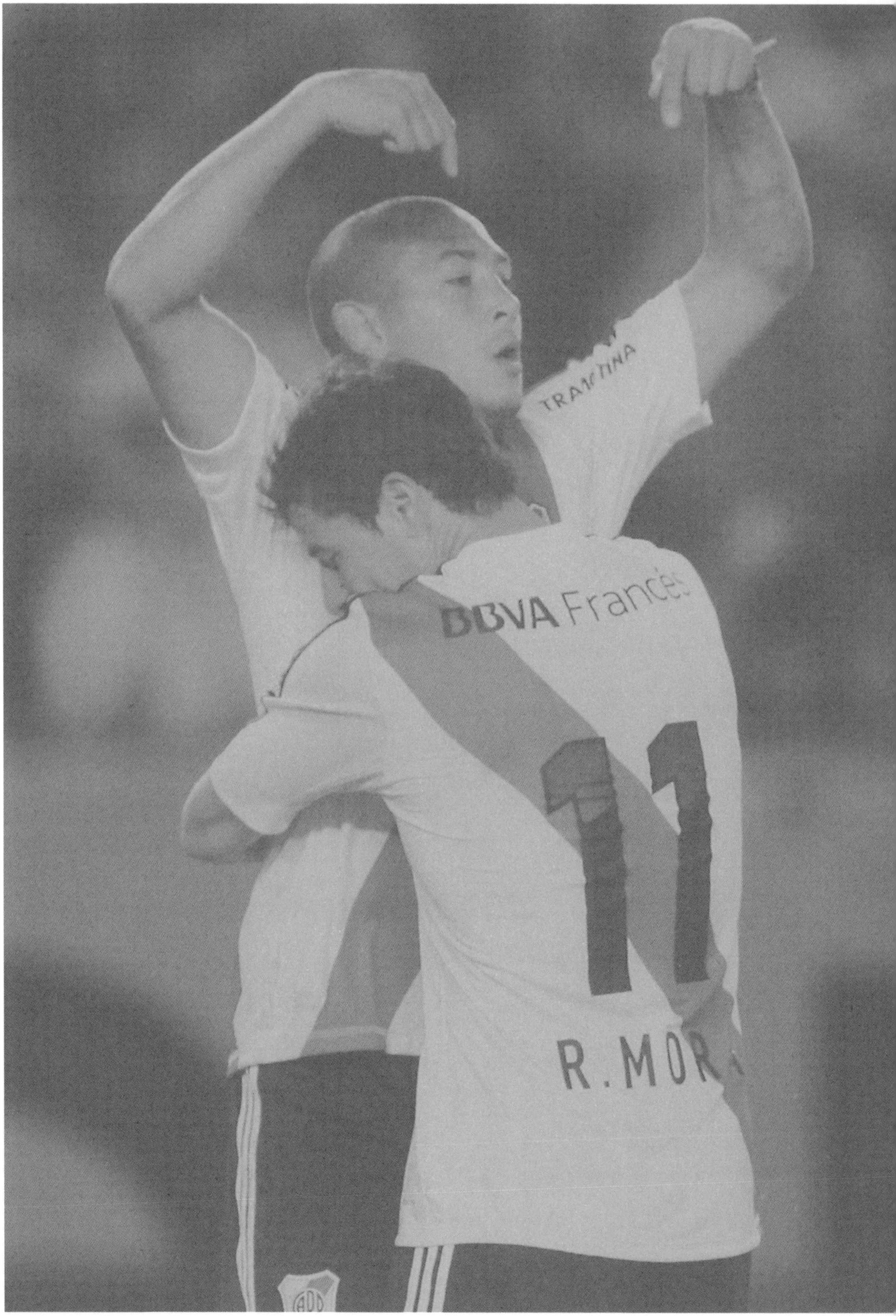
BBVA Francés
11

Spain
Germany
Italy
England
France
Netherlands
Denmark
Sweden
Portugal
Russia
Belgium
Greece
Switzerland
Ukraine
Israel
Norway

785
Football Shirts from
Around
the World

Brazil
Mexico
United States
Argentina
Colombia
Uruguay
Chile
Ecuador
Ivory Coast
South Africa
Morocco
...

Around the world in 785 jerseys

n the early days of the Beautiful Game, players' shirts were not what they are today. Scraps of wool that distinguished one team from another, they were merely a tool, like ankle-high boots with studs and long shorts. The only objects that directly represented a club back then were vague novelties and souvenirs.

Football historians have traced the emergence of the first equipment manufacturer back to 1879, before the advent of the professional game. That first manufacturer, Bukta, moved offices to Manchester, in the north of England, in 1885, when lighter cotton shirts began to replace the heavy, unsuitable wool.

It took some time to understand the potential commercial benefits of selling football shirts. They gradually became a way for fans to identify with a club. Wearing such-and-such a jersey was a statement, a courageous commitment, especially in a town or city with more than one club. It also enabled a fan to adopt another persona, to forget their humdrum routine, to be, in a very real sense, a part of the club.

A source of countless fantasies, jerseys finally won over suppliers in 1977, the year shirt sponsorship was approved by the English FA and football is said to have entered its modern age. Since then, football shirts have been transformed into flagship products for brands and lucrative spin-off items for clubs. Manufacturers are constantly redesigning the shirts in the name of merchandising. More appealing, more abundant, more expensive, and coveted throughout the world. Be they collectors' items for aficionados or products to be auctioned online, jerseys have become the golden goose for passionate football fans—and for those businessmen keen to make money catering to them.

The jersey is now sometimes more important than the player. It is not unusual for a club to buy a player based on how many replica jerseys he is likely to sell rather than his ability on the field. It is a piece of kit that has transformed into a fashion accessory.

But, thankfully, the magic remains. Fans watch over a jersey, defending it like guardians of a sacred temple. They feverishly wait for the new version each season, and some dispute the slightest change, considered an affront to the original colours and crest. Football shirts say much about our culture—that's why they fascinate us and differ from one corner of the globe to the next. And this is why the topic deserves a round-the-world overview. Bon voyage, and don't forget your shirt!

the best sellers

clubs selling the most shirts

(2018; source : Euromericas Sport Marketing)

Manchester United (England)
3.25 million

Real Madrid (Spain)
3.12 million

Bayern Munich (Germany)
2.58 million

FC Barcelona (Spain)
1.93 million

Liverpool (England)
1.67 million

Juventus (Italy)
1.62 million

Chelsea (England)
1.53 million

**Borussia Dortmund
(Germany)**
1.21 million

Paris SG (France)
1.5 million

Manchester City (England)
1.09 million

the best paid

clubs with the biggest contracts from equipment manufacturers **(during 2019–2020 season, source: L'équipe)**

FC Barcelona (Spain)
€155 M per year – Nike
(until 2028)

Real Madrid (Spain)
€120 M – Adidas
(until 2028)

**Manchester United
(England)**
€95 M – Adidas
(until 2025)

Paris SG (France)
€80 M – Nike
(until 2032)

Manchester City (England)
€75 M – Puma
(until 2029)

Arsenal (England)
€70 M – Adidas
(until 2024)

the most expensive

clubs with the biggest sponsorship deals
(during 2019–20 season, source: L'équipe)

Real Madrid (Spain)
€70 M per year
Fly Emirates

Manchester United (England)
€68 M – Chevrolet

FC Barcelona (Spain)
€55 M – Rakuten

Paris SG (France)
€52 M –All Accor
Live Limitless

Manchester City (England)
€52 M – Etihad Airways

Arsenal (England)
€50 M – Fly Emirates

memorial shirts

in memory of those who have died

Paris SG (France)
Je suis Paris
November 2015

AS Saint-Étienne (France)
Pray for Paris
November 2015

**Hamilton Academical
(Scotland)**
Homage to the victims
of the Paris attacks
November 2015

OGC Nice (France)
Heart shirt
August 2016

Serie A (Italy)
Genoa in our hearts
August 2018

RC Strasbourg (France)
Strasbourg, mon amour
December 2018

Paris SG (France)
Notre-Dame
April 2019

FC Barcelona (Spain)
Gràcies Johan
April 2016

Corinthians (Brazil)
Magic Senna
October 2018

Bohemian FC (Ireland)
Bob Marley
October 2018

so special

when clubs celebrate their birthdays

Juventus (Italy)
1997 – centenary

Olympique de Marseille (France)
1998 – centenary

FC Barcelona (Spain)
1999 – centenary

Arsenal (England)
2006 – Highbury
1913-2006

Inter Milan (Italy)
2008 – centenary

Corinthians (Brazil)
2010 – centenary

Lazio (Italy)
2010
110 years, third

Paris SG (France)
2011 – 40 years

Fluminense (Brazil)
2012 – 110 years

Santos (Brazil)
2012
centenary, third

Celtic FC (Scotland)
2013
125 years, third

Genoa (Italy)
2013
centenary, away

United States (national team)
2013 – centenary

PSV Eindhoven (Netherlands)
2014
centenary, away

Manchester City (England)
2019 – 125 years

so wild

when designers let themselves go

**Colorado Caribous
(United States)**
1978

Ajax Amsterdam (Netherlands)
1990 – away

Australia (national team)
1991

**Manchester United
(England)**
1991 – away

Arsenal (England)
1992 – away

**Queens Park Rangers
(England)**
1992 – goalkeeper

Reading (England)
1992 – away

Atalanta Bergamasca (Italy)
1994 – away

Bristol Rovers (England)
1994 – away

Derby County (England)
1994 – away

Hull City (England)
1994

Madureira (Brazil)
1994

Shamrock Rovers (Ireland)
1994 – away

Chelsea (England)
1995 – away

Notts County (England)
1995 – away

Scunthorpe United (England)
1995 – away

Croatia (national team)
1996 – goalkeeper

England (national team)
1996 – goalkeeper

FC Barcelona (Spain)
1997 – away

**Manchester United
(England)**
1998 – goalkeeper

Mexico (national team)
1998

Bochum (Germany)
1998

Mexico (national team)
1999 –goalkeeper

Jaguares de Chiapas (Mexico)
2003

Athletic Bilbao (Spain)
2004

AS Saint-Étienne (France)
2005 – goalkeeper

Olympique de Marseille (France)
2008 – away

Olympique Lyonnais (France)
2011 – away

Everton (England)
2012 – goalkeeper

Charleroi SC (Belgium)
2013

Recreativo de Huelva (Spain)
2013 – away

FC Rostov (Russia)
2019 – fourth

SC Braga (Portugal)
2020 – third

so vintage

jerseys from days of old

Juventus (Italy)
1898

FC Barcelona (Spain)
1903

Chelsea (England)
1905

Boca Juniors (Argentina)
1907

Boca Juniors (Argentina)
1908

Borussia Dortmund (Germany)
1909

Santos (Brazil)
1912

Fluminense (Brazil)
1940

Monterrey (Mexico)
1945

Vélez Sarsfield (Argentina)
1945

**South Africa
(national team)**
1947

Jamaica (national team)
1948

Spain (national team)
1950

United States (national team)
1950

**Dukla Prague
(Czech republic)**
1960

AS Monaco (France)
1961

Cuba (national team)
1962

AS Roma (Italy)
1966

USSR (national team)
1966

Congo (national team)
1968

Parme (Italy)
1969

SSD Palermo (Italy)
1970 (away)

Albania (national team)
1973

GDR (national team)
1974

Japan (national team)
1974

Netherlands (national team)
1974

AS Saint-Étienne (France)
1976

**Los Angeles Aztecs
(United States)**
1976

**Northern Ireland
(national team)**
1977

SC Bastia (France)
1978

Chemnitzer FC (Germany)
1978

Guatemala (national team)
1978

**Tampa Bay Rowdies
(United States)**
1978

**Fort Lauderdale Strikers
(United States)**
1979

**New England Tea Men
(United States)**
1979

**California Surf
(United States)**
1980 – away

Ghana (national team)
1980

Mali (national team)
1980

**Mozambique
(national team)**
1980

Suriname (national team)
1980

Montreal Manic (Canada)
1981

Mexico (national team)
1982 – away

From Argentina to Zambia, a journey across Planet Football

United States
Winner
Nike

Netherlands
Runners-up
Nike

Sweden
Semifinalist (third)
Adidas

England
Semifinalist (fourth)
Nike

Norway
Quarterfinalist
Nike

France
Quarterfinalist
Nike

Italy
Quarterfinalist
Puma

Germany
Quarterfinalist
Adidas

Nigeria
Eighth finalist
Nike

Australia
Eighth finalist
Nike

Cameroon
Eighth finalist
Le Coq Sportif

Brazil
Eighth finalist
Nike

Spain
Eighth finalist
Adidas

Canada
Eighth finalist
Nike

China
Eighth finalist
Nike

Japan
Eighth finalist
Adidas

South Korea
First round
Nike

South Africa
First round
Nike

Jamaica
First round
Umbro

Argentina
First round
Adidas

Scotland
First round
Adidas

New Zealand
First round
Nike

Chile
First round
Nike

Thailand
First round
Warrlx

Copa América 2019

6 jerseys of the 46th edition of the tournament

Brazil
Winner –
Nike

Peru
Runners-up –
Marathon

Argentina
Semifinalist (third)
Adidas

Chile
Semifinalist (fourth)
Nike

Colombia
Quarterfinalist
Adidas

Uruguay
Quarterfinalist
Puma

Africa Cup of Nations 2019

6 jerseys from the 32nd edition of the Africa Cup of Nations

Algeria
Winner
Adidas

Senegal
Runners-up
Puma

Nigeria
Semifinalist (third)
Nike

Tunisia
Semifinalist (fourth)
Kappa

South Africa
Quarterfinalist
Nike

Ivory Coast
Quarterfinalist
Puma

UEFA Euro 2020

24 jerseys from the teams participating in the UEFA Euro

Germany
2020 – Adidas

Germany
2019 – away – Adidas

France
2019 – Nike

France
2019 – away – Nike

Netherlands
2019 – Nike

Netherlands
2019 – away – Nike

England
2019 – Nike

England
2019 – away – Nike

Spain
2020 – Adidas

Italy
2019 – Puma

Denmark
2019 – Hummel

Portugal
2019 – Nike

Russia
2020 – Adidas

Ukraine
2019 – Joma

Czech Republic
2019 – Puma

Austria
2019 – Puma

Belgium
2020 – Adidas

Croatia
2019 – Nike

Finland
2019 – Nike

Wales
2020 – Adidas

Poland
2019 – Nike

Sweden
2020 – Adidas

Switzerland
2019 – Puma

Turkey
2019 – Nike

England

National team
2019 – Nike

National team
2019 – away – Nike

Arsenal
2020 – Adidas

Arsenal
2020 – away – Adidas

Aston Villa
2020 – Kappa

Blackburn Rovers
2020 – Umbro

AFC Bournemouth
2020 – Umbro

Brighton & Hove Albion
2020 – Nike

Burnley
2020 – Umbro

Chelsea
2020 – Nike

Chelsea
2020 – away – Nike

Crystal Palace
2020 – Puma

Derby County
2020 – Umbro

Everton
2020 – Umbro

Leeds United
2020 – Kappa

Leicester City
2020 – Adidas

Liverpool
2020 – New Balance

Liverpool
2020 – away
New Balance

Manchester City
2020 – Puma

Manchester City
2020– away – Puma

Manchester United
2020 – Adidas

Manchester United
2020 – away – Adidas

Newcastle United
2020 – Puma

Norwich City
2020 – Erreà

Nottingham Forest
2020 – Macron

Sheffield United
2020 – Adidas

Southampton
2020 – Under Armour

Sunderland
2020 – Adidas

Tottenham Hotspur
2020 – Nike

Tottenham Hotspur
2020 – away – Nike

Watford
2020 – Adidas

West Ham United
2020 – Umbro

Wolverhampton Wanderers
2020 – Adidas

Spain

National team
2019 – Adidas

National team
2019 – away – Adidas

Athletic Bilbao
2020 – New Balance

Athletic Bilbao
2020 – away
New Balance

Atlético Madrid
2020 – Nike

Atlético Madrid
2020 – away – Nike

FC Barcelona
2020 – Nike

FC Barcelona
2020 – away – Nike

FC Barcelona
2020 (third) – Nike

Real Betis
2020 – Kappa

Celta Vigo
2020 – Adidas

Deportivo Alavés
2020 – Kelme

Deportivo de La Coruña
2020 – Macron

SD Eibar
2020 – Joma

Espanyol de Barcelona
2020 – Kelme

Getafe CF
2020 – Joma

Grenade CF
2020 – Nike

CD Leganés
2020 – Joma

Levante UD
2020 – Macron

RCD Mallorca
2020 – Umbro

Málaga CF
2020 – Nike

CA Osasuna
2020 – Hummel

Real Madrid
2020 – Adidas

Real Madrid
2020– away – Adidas

Real Madrid
2020 (third) – Adidas

Real Zaragoza
2020 – Adidas

Real Sociedad
2020 – Macron

Real Valladolid
2020 – Adidas

Sevilla FC
2020 – Nike

Sevilla FC
2020 – away – Nike

Valencia CF
2020 – Puma

Valencia CF
2020 – away – Puma

Villarreal CF
2020 – Joma

Germany

National team
2019 – Adidas

National team
2019 – away – Adidas

FC Augsbourg
2020 – Nike

Hertha BSC
2020 – Nike

FC Union Berlin
2020 – Macron

Borussia Dortmund
2020 – Puma

Borussia Dortmund
2020 – away – Puma

Borussia Dortmund
2020 (third) – Puma

Borussia Mönchengladbach
2020 – Puma

Borussia Mönchengladbach
2020 – away – Puma

Bayer 04 Leverkusen
2020 – Jako

Bayer 04 Leverkusen
2020 – away – Jako

Bayern Munich
2020 – Adidas

Bayern Munich
2020 – away– Adidas

Bayern Munich
2020 (third) – Adidas

FC Cologne
2020 – Uhlsport

Fortuna Düsseldorf
2020 – Uhlsport

Eintracht Frankfurt
2020 – Nike

SC Fribourg
2020 – Hummel

Hamburger SV
2020 – Adidas

Hamburger SV
2020 – away – Adidas

TSG 1899 Hoffenheim
2020 – Joma

RB Leipzig
2020 – Nike

RB Leipzig
2020 – away – Nike

FSV Mainz 05
2020 – Lotto

SC Paderborn 07
2020 – Saller

Schalke 04
2020 – Umbro

Schalke 04
2020 – away – Umbro

VfB Stuttgart
2020 – Jako

VfL Wolfsburg
2020 – Nike

VfL Wolfsburg
2020 – away – Nike

Werder Bremen
2020 – Umbro

Werder Bremen
2020 – away – Umbro

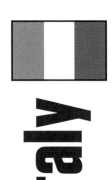

Italy

National team
2019 – Puma

National team
2019 – away – Puma

Atalanta BC
2020 – Joma

Bologna FC
2020 – Macron

Brescia
2020 – Kappa

Cagliari
2020 – Macron

ACF Fiorentina
2020 – Le Coq Sportif

ACF Fiorentina
2020 – away –
Le Coq Sportif

Genoa FC
2020 – Kappa

FC Inter Milan
2020 – Nike

FC Inter Milan
2020 – away – Nike

FC Inter Milan
2020 (third) – Nike

Juventus FC
2020 – Adidas

Juventus FC
2020 – away – Adidas

Juventus FC
2020 (third) – Adidas

SS Lazio
2020 – Macron

SS Lazio
2020 – away – Macron

U.S. Lecce
2020 – M908

AC Milan
2020 – Puma

AC Milan
2020 – away – Puma

AC Milan
2020 (third) – Puma

SSC Napoli
2020 – Kappa

SSC Napoli
2020 – away – Kappa

SSC Napoli
2020 (third) – Kappa

Parma
2020 – Erreà

AS Roma
2020 – Nike

AS Roma
2020 – away – Nike

Sampdoria
2020 – Joma

U.S. Sassuolo
2020 – Kappa

Spal
2020 – Macron

Torino FC
2020 – Joma

Udinese
2020 – Macron

Hellas Verona FC
2020 – Macron

France

National team
2019 – Nike

National team
2019 – away – Nike

Amiens SC
2020 – Puma

Angers SCO
2020 – Kappa

Girondins de Bordeaux
2020 – Puma

Girondins de Bordeaux
2020 – away – Puma

Stade Brestois 29
2020 – Nike

Dijon FCO
2020 – Lotto

RC Lens
2020 – Macron

LOSC Lille
2020 – New Balance

LOSC Lille
2020 – away
New Balance

Olympique Lyonnais
2020 – Adidas

Olympique Lyonnais
2020 – away – Adidas

Olympique de Marseille
2020 – Puma

Olympique de Marseille
2020 – away – Puma

Olympique de Marseille
2020 (third) – Puma

FC Metz
2020 – Nike

AS Monaco FC
2020 – Kappa

AS Monaco FC
2020 – away – Kappa

Montpellier Hérault SC
2020 – Nike

FC Nantes
2020 – New Balance

FC Nantes
2020 – away –
New Balance

OGC Nice
2020 – Macron

Nîmes Olympique
2020 – Puma

Stade de Reims
2020 – Umbro

Stade Rennais FC
2020 – Puma

Paris SG FC
2020 – Nike

Paris SG FC
2020 – away – Nike

Paris SG FC
2020 (third) – Nike

AS Saint-Étienne
2020 – Le Coq Sportif

AS Saint-Étienne
2020 – away
Le Coq Sportif

RC Strasbourg
2020 – Adidas

Toulouse FC
2020 – Joma

Netherlands

National team
2019 – Nike

National team
2019 – away – Nike

AZ Alkmaar
2020 – Under Armour

Heracles Almelo
2020 – Acerbis

Ajax Amsterdam
2020 – Adidas

Vitesse Arnhem
2020 – Nike

PSV Eindhoven
2020 – Umbro

FC Groningen
2020 – Puma

Sportclub Heerenveen
2020 – Jako

ADO Den Haag
2020 – Erreà

Feyenoord Rotterdam
2020 – Adidas

Willem II Tilburg
2020 – Robey

FC Twente
2020 – Kick's 21

FC Utrecht
2020 – Nike

PEC Zwolle
2020 – Craft

Belgium

National team
2019 – Adidas

National team
2019 – away – Adidas

RSC Anderlecht
2020 – Joma

Royal Antwerp FC
2020 – Jako

Cercle Brugge KSV
2020 – Kappa

Club Brugge KV
2020 – Macron

Charleroi SC
2020 – Kappa

KV Kortrijk
2020 – Beltona

KAS Eupen
2020 – Nike

KRC Genk
2020 – Nike

KAA Gent
2020 – Craft

Standard Liège
2020 – New Balance

KV Mechelen
2020 – Jartazi

Royal Excel Mouscron
2020 – Uhlsport

Zulte Waregem
2020 – Patrick

Portugal

National team
2019 – Nike

National team
2019 – away – Nike

Os Belenenses
2020 – Lacatoni

Benfica
2020 – Adidas

Benfica
2020 – away – Adidas

Boavista FC
2020 – PlayGround Stars

SC Braga
2020 – Hummel

Gil Vicente FC
2020 – Lacatoni

FC Paços de Ferreira
2020 – Joma

FC Porto
2020 – New Balance

FC Porto
2020 – away –
New Balance

Rio Ave FC
2020 – Nike

Sporting CP
2020 – Macron

Vitória Guimarães
2020 – Macron

Vitória Setúbal
2020 – Hummel

Russia

National team
2019 – Adidas

National team
2019 – away – Adidas

FC Arsenal Tula
2020 – Adidas

Akhmat Grozny
2020 – Adidas

CSKA Moscow
2020 – Umbro

FC Dynamo Moscow
2020 – Kelme

FC Krasnodar
2020 – Puma

Lokomotiv Moscow
2020 – Under Armour

FC Ufa
2020 – Joma

FC Ural Yekaterinburg
2020 – Adidas

FC Rostov
2020 – Adidas

FC Rubin Kazan
2020 – Jako

PFC Sochi
2020 – Nike

Spartak Moscow
2020 – Nike

Zenit Saint Petersburg
2020 – Nike

Sweden

National team
2019 – Adidas

National team
2019 – away – Adidas

AIK Fotboll
2020 – Nike

BK Häcken
2020 – Puma

Djurgårdens IF
2020 – Adidas

IF Elfsborg
2020 – Umbro

IFK Göteborg
2020 – Kappa

Hammarby IF
2020 – Craft

Kalmar FF
2020 – Hummel

Malmö FF
2020 – Puma

IFK Norrköping
2020 – Nike

Örebro SK
2020 – Puma

Östersunds FK
2020 – Adidas

IK Sirius
2020 – Nike

GIF Sundsvall
2020 – Adidas

Denmark

National team
2019 – Hummel

National team
2019 – away – Hummel

AaB Aalborg
2020 – Hummel

AGF Aarhus
2020 – Hummel

Brøndby IF
2020 – Hummel

FC Copenhagen
2020 – Adidas

Esbjerg fB
2020 – Nike

Hobro IK
2020 – Puma

AC Horsens
2020 – Hummel

FC Midtjylland
2020 – Nike

FC Nordsjælland
2020 – Nike

Odense Boldklub
2020 – Hummel

Randers FC
2020 – Puma

Silkeborg IF
2020 – Uhlsport

SønderjyskE
2020 – Hummel

(Europe continued)

Croatia
2019 – Nike

Switzerland
2019 – Puma

Poland
2019 – Nike

Wales
2019 – Adidas

Ukraine
2019 – Joma

Austria
2019 – Puma

Ireland
2019 – New Balance

Serbia
2019 – Puma

Turkey
2019 – Nike

Iceland
2019 – Erreà

Czech Republic
2019 – Puma

Norway
2019 – Nike

Scotland
2019 – Adidas

Finland
2019 – Nike

Greece
2019 – Nike

Dinamo Zagreb (Croatia)
2020 – Adidas

FC Basel (Switzerland)
2020 – Adidas

**BSC Young Boys
(Switzerland)**
2020 – Nike

FC Shakhtar Donetsk (Ukraine)
2020 – Nike

Dynamo Kiev (Ukraine)
2020 – New Balance

FC RB Salzburg (Austria)
2020 – Nike

Red Star Belgrade (Serbia)
2020 – Macron

Fenerbahçe (Turkey)
2020 – Adidas

Galatasaray (Turkey)
2020 – Nike

**Slavia Prague
(Czech Republic)**
2020 – Puma

**Sparta Prague
(Czech Republic)**
2020 – Nike

Rosenborg BK (Norway)
2020 – Adidas

Celtic FC (Scotland)
2020 – New Balance

Rangers FC (Scotland)
2020 – Hummel

HJK Helsinki (Finland)
2020 – Adidas

Olympiakos (Greece)
2020 – Adidas

Panathinaïkos (Greece)
2020 – Kappa

Steaua (Romania)
2020 – Nike

Brazil

National team
2019 – Nike

National team
2019 (away) – Nike

Alagoano
2019 – Azulão

Bahia
2019 – Esquadrão

Bahia
2019 – away –
Esquadrão

Botafogo
2019 – Topper

Ceará
2019 – Topper

Chapecoense
2019 – Umbro

Corinthians
2019 – Nike

Corinthians
2019 – away – Nike

Coritiba
2019 – 1909 Sports

Cruzeiro
2019 – Umbro

Flamengo
2019 – Adidas

Flamengo
2019 – away – Adidas

Fluminense FC
2019 – Under Armour

Fluminense
2019 – away –
Under Armour

Fortaleza
2019 – Leão 1918

Goiás
2019 – Gr33n

Grêmio
2019 – Umbro

Grêmio
2019 – away – Umbro

SC Internacional
2019 – Nike

SC Internacional
2019 – away – Nike

Atlético Mineiro
2019 – Le Coq Sportif

Atlético Mineiro
2019 – away –
Le Coq Sportif

Palmeiras
2019 – Puma

Palmeiras
2019 – away – Puma

Paranaense
2019 – Umbro

Santos FC
2019 – Umbro

Santos FC
2019 – away – Umbro

São Paulo FC
2019 – Adidas

São Paulo FC
2019 – away – Adidas

CR Vasco da Gama
2019 – Diadora

CR Vasco da Gama
2019 –away – Diadora

Argentina

National team
2019 – Adidas

National team
2019 (away) – Adidas

Aldosivi
2020 – Kappa

Argentinos Juniors
2020 – Umbro

Arsenal de Sarandí
2020 – Lyon

Banfield
2020 – Hummel

Boca Juniors
2020 – Nike

Boca Juniors
2020 (away) – Nike

Central Córdoba
2020 – Adhoc

CA Colón
2020 – Kelme

Defensa y Justicia
2020 – Lyon

Estudiantes de La Plata
2020 – Under Armour

Gimnasia y Esgrima
2020 – Le Coq Sportif

Godoy Cruz
2020 – Kelme

CA Huracán
2020 – TBS

Independiente
2020 – Puma

Independiente
2020 – away – Puma

Lanús
2020 – Peak

Newell's Old Boys
2020 – Umbro

Newell's Old Boys
2020 – away – Umbro

Patronato
2020 – Lyon

Racing Club
2020 – Kappa

Racing Club
2020 – away – Kappa

River Plate
2020 – Adidas

River Plate
2020 – away – Adidas

Rosario Central
2020 – Under Armour

San Lorenzo de Almagro
2020 – Nike

San Lorenzo de Almagro
2020 – away – Nike

Talleres
2020 – Givova

Atlético Tucumán
2020 – Umbro

Unión de Santa Fe
2020 – Kappa

Vélez Sarsfield
2020 – Kappa

Vélez Sarsfield
2020 – away – Kappa

Uruguay

National team
2019 – Puma

National team
2019 – away – Puma

Club Nacional
2019 – Umbro

Danubio FC
2019 – Luanvi

Defensor SC
2019 – Umbro

Peñarol
2019 – Puma

Chile

National team
2019 – Nike

National team
2019 – away – Nike

Colo-Colo
2019 – Umbro

Unión Española
2019 – Kappa

Universidad Católica
2019 – Under Armour

Universidad de Chile
2019 – Adidas

Colombia

National team
2019 – Adidas

National team
2019 – away – Adidas

América de Cali
2019 – Umbro

Atlético Nacional
2019 – Nike

Millonarios FC
2019 – Adidas

Once Caldas
2019 – Erreà

Ecuador

National team
2019 – Marathon

National team
2019 –away – Marathon

Barcelona SC
2019 – Marathon

El Nacional
2019 – Lotto

CS Emelec
2019 – Adidas

LDU Quito
2019 – Puma

Mexico

National team
2019 – Adidas

National team
2019 – away – Adidas

Club América
2019 – Nike

Club América
2019 – away – Nike

Atlante FC
2019 – Kappa

Atlas FC
2019 – Adidas

CD Guadalajara
2019 – Puma

CD Guadalajara
2019 – away – Puma

Club León
2019 – Pirma

Club León
2019 – away – Pirma

Cruz Azul
2019 – Joma

Cruz Azul
2019 – away – Joma

Deportivo Toluca
2019 – Under Armour

Deportivo Toluca
2019 – away –
Under Armour

Dorados de Sinaloa
2019 – Charly

Lobos BUAP
2019 – Pirma

Monarcas Morelia
2019 – Pirma

Monterrey
2019 – Puma

Necaxa
2019 – Charly

CF Pachuca
2019 – Charly

CF Pachuca
2019 – away – Charly

Club Puebla
2019 – Umbro

Pumas UNAM
2019 – Nike

Pumas UNAM
2019 – away – Nike

Querétaro FC
2019 – Puma

Atlético San Luis
2019 – Pirma

Santos Laguna
2019 – Charly

Santos Laguna
2019 – away – Charly

Tiburones Rojos de Veracruz
2019 – Charly

Tigres UANL
2019 – Adidas

Tigres UANL
2019 – away – Adidas

Club Tijuana
2019 – Charly

Universidad de Guadalajara
2019 – Umbro

United States

National team
2019 – Nike

National team
2019 – away – Nike

Atlanta United
2019 – Adidas

Chicago Fire
2019 – Adidas

FC Cincinnati
2019 – Adidas

Colorado Rapids
2019 – Adidas

Columbus Crew
2019 – Adidas

FC Dallas
2019 – Adidas

Houston Dynamo
2019 – Adidas

Los Angeles FC
2019 – Adidas

Los Angeles Galaxy
2019 – Adidas

Los Angeles Galaxy
2019 – away – Adidas

Minnesota United
2019 – Adidas

New England Revolution
2019 – Adidas

New York City FC
2019 – Adidas

New York RB
2019 – Adidas

Orlando City SC
2019 – Adidas

Philadelphia Union
2019 – Adidas

Portland Timbers
2019 – Adidas

Real Salt Lake
2019 – Adidas

San José Earthquakes
2019 – Adidas

Seattle Sounders
2019 – Adidas

Sporting Kansas City
2019 – Adidas

DC United
2019 – Adidas

Canada

National team
2019 – Nike

National team
2019 – away – Nike

Toronto FC
2019 – Adidas

Toronto FC
2019 – away – Adidas

Montreal Impact
2019 – Adidas

Vancouver Whitecaps FC
2019 – Adidas

Paraguay (national team)
2019 – Adidas

Club Olimpia (Paraguay)
2019 – Adidas

Bolivia (national team)
2019 – Marathon

Venezuela (national team)
2019 – Givova

Costa Rica (national team)
2019 – New Balance

**Deportivo Saprissa
(Costa Rica)**
2019 – Kappa

Honduras (national team)
2019 – Joma

CD Olimpia (Honduras)
2019 – Umbro

Guatemala (national team)
2019 – Umbro

Nicaragua (national team)
2019 – Joma

El Salvador (national team)
2019 – Umbro

Alianza FC (El Salvador)
2019 – Umbro

Panama (national team)
2019 – New Balance

Haiti (national team)
2019 – Saeta

Jamaica (national team)
2019 – Umbro

Tunisia

National team
2019 – Kappa

National team
2019 – away – Kappa

Club Africain
2019 – Umbro

Étoile du Sahel
2019 – Macron

CS Sfaxien
2019 – Macron

ES Tunis
2019 – Umbro

Morocco

National team
2019 – Adidas

National team
2019 – away – Adidas

Raja Casablanca
2019 – Legea

Wydad AC
2019 – Macron

Royal Army Club
2019 – Joma

Ittihad Tanger
2019 – Gloria

Egypt

National team
2019 – Puma

National team
2019 – away – Puma

Al Ahly SC
2019 – Umbro

Ismaily SC
2019 – Jako

Pyramids SC
2019 – Kappa

Zamalek SC
2019 – Puma

Algeria

National team
2019 – Adidas

National team
2019 – away – Adidas

USM Alger
2019 – Joma

CS Constantine
2019 – Joma

JS Kabylie
2019 – Macron

ES Sétif
2019 – Joma

South Africa

National team
2019 – Nike

National team
2019 (away) – Nike

AmaZulu FC
2019 – Umbro

BidVest Wits
2019 – Kappa

Bloemfontein Celtic
2019 – Umbro

Cape Town City
2019 – Umbro

Cape Town City
2019 (away) – Umbro

Chippa United
2019 – Umbro

Kaizer Chiefs
2019 – Nike

Kaizer Chiefs
2019 (away) – Nike

Mamelodi Sundowns
2019 – Puma

Mamelodi Sundowns
2019 (away) – Puma

Maritzburg United
2019 – Lotto

Orlando Pirates
2019 – Adidas

Orlando Pirates
2019 (away) – Adidas

Angola (national team)
2019 – Lacatoni

Angola (national team)
2019 – away – Lacatoni

Benign (national team)
2019 – Umbro

Burundi (national team)
2019 – Garman

Cameroon (national team)
2019 – Le Coq Sportif

Cameroon (national team)
2019 – away –
Le Coq Sportif

DR Congo (national team)
2019 – O'Neills

DR Congo (national team)
2019 – away – O'Neills

TP Mazembe (DR Congo)
2019 – Sogam

TP Mazembe (DR Congo)
2019 – away – Sogam

**Ivory Coast
(national team)**
2019 – Puma

**Ivory Coast
(national team)**
2019 – away – Puma

Ghana (national team)
2019 – Puma

Ghana (national team)
2019 – away – Puma

Asante Kotoko (Ghana)
2019 – Strike

Guinea (national team)
2019 – Macron

Guinea (national team)
2019 – away – Macron

Kenya (national team)
2019 – Macron

**Madagascar
(national team)**
2019 – Garman

**Madagascar
(national team)**
2019 – away – Garman

Mali (national team)
2019 – Airness

Mali (national team)
2019 – away – Airness

Mauritania (national team)
2019 – AB Sport

Nigeria (national team)
2019 – Nike

Nigeria (national team)
2019 – away – Nike

Ouganda (national team)
2019 – Mafro Sports

Ouganda (national team)
2019 – away –
Mafro Sports

Senegal (national team)
2019 – Puma

Senegal (national team)
2019 – away – Puma

Tanzania (national team)
2019 – Uhlsport

Zambia (national team)
2019 – Mafro Sports

Zesco United (Zambia)
2019 – Umbro

Zimbabwe (national team)
2019 – Umbro

Japan

National team
2019 – Adidas

National team
2019 – away – Adidas

Sanfrecce Hiroshima
2019 – Nike

Kashima Antlers
2019 – Nike

Kawasaki Frontale
2019 – Puma

Vissel Kobe
2019 – Asics

Nagoya Grampus
2019 – Mizuno

Oita Trinita
2019 – Puma

Gamba Osaka
2019 – Umbro

Consadole Sapporo
2019 – Kappa

Vegalta Sendai
2019 – Adidas

FC Tokyo
2019 – Umbro

Sagan Tosu
2019 – New Balance

Urawa Red Diamonds
2019 – Nike

Yokohama F. Marinos
2019 – Adidas

South Korea

National team
2019 – Nike

National team
2019 – away – Nike

Daegu FC
2019 – Forward

Gangwon FC
2019 – Puma

Gyeongnam FC
2019 – Hummel

Incheon United FC
2019 – Hummel

Jeju United FC
2019 – Kika

Jeonbuk Hyundai Motors FC
2019 – Hummel

Jeonbuk Hyundai Motors FC
2019 – away –
Hummel

Pohang Steelers
2019 – Astore

Seongnam FC
2019 – Umbro

Seongnam FC
2019 – away
Umbro

FC Seoul
2019 – Le Coq Sportif

Suwon Samsung Bluewings
2019 – Puma

Ulsan Hyundai FC
2019 – Hummel

Australia

National team
2019 – Nike

National team
2019 – away – Nike

Adélaïde United
2019 – Macron

Brisbane Roar
2019 – Umbro

Brisbane Roar
2019 – away – Umbro

Central Coast Mariners
2019 – Umbro

Melbourne City FC
2019 – Puma

Melbourne Victory
2019 – Adidas

Melbourne Victory
2019 – away –
Adidas

Newcastle United Jets
2019 – Viva

Perth Glory FC
2019 – Macron

Sydney FC
2019 – Puma

Sydney FC
2019 – away – Puma

Western Sydney Wanderers
2019 – Nike

Wellington Phoenix
(New Zealand franchise
engaged in A-League)
2019 – Adidas

China

National team
2019 – Nike

National team
2019 – away – Nike

Beijing Guoan
2019 – Nike

Beijing Renhe FC
2019 – Nike

Chongqing Lifan
2019 – Nike

Dalian Yifang FC
2019 – Nike

Guangzhou Evergrande
2019 – Nike

Guangzhou R&F
2019 – Nike

Hebei China Fortune
2019 – Nike

Henan Jianye
2019 – Nike

Jiangsu Suning
2019 – Nike

Shandong Luneng Taishan
2019 – Nike

Shanghai Greenland Shenhua
2019 – Nike

Shanghai SIPG
2019 – Nike

Tianjin Tianhai
2019 – Nike

**Saudi Arabia
(national team)**
2019 – Nike

Al-Hilal (Saudi Arabia)
2019 – Mouj

Iran (national team)
2019 – Uhlsport

Esteghlal FC (Iran)
2019 – Li Ning

Qatar (national team)
2019 – Nike

Al Sadd SC (Qatar)
2019 – Puma

United Arab Emirates
(national team)
2019 – Adidas

Bahreïn
(national team)
2019 – Macron

Afghanistan
(national team)
2019 – Hummel

Turkmenistan
(national team)
2019 – Jako

Uzbekistan
(national team)
2019 – Jako

India
(national team)
2019 – Six5Six

Thailand
(national team)
2019 – Warrix

Malaysia
(national team)
2019 – Nike

Vietnam
(national team)
2019 – Grand Sport

Index by club names

A

Table of contents

Picture credits